super
boosters

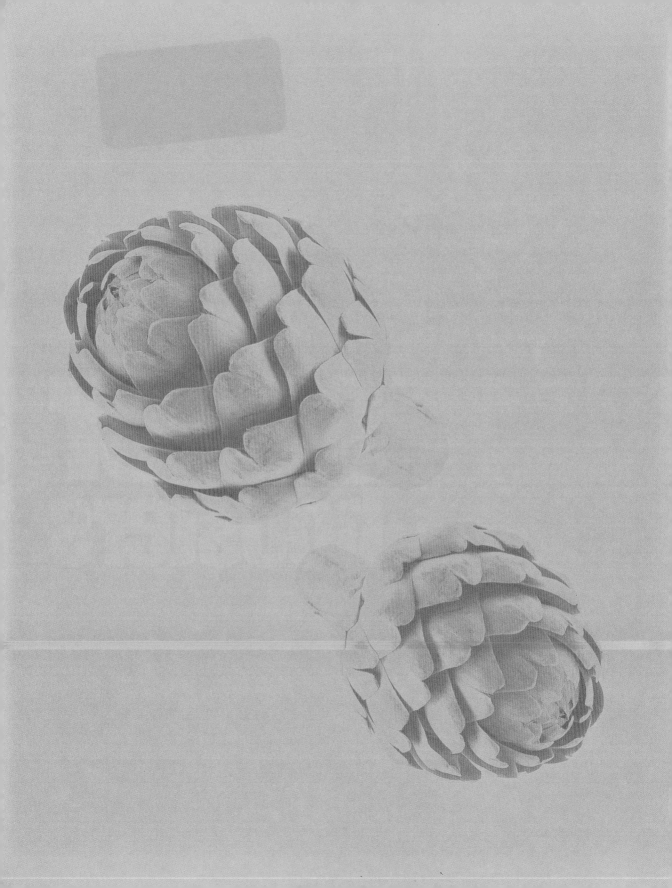

michael van straten

super boosters

herb, plant & spice extracts to boost health

Dedication

With thanks as always to the entire Mitchell Beazley staff, especially to Becca, who took over the project long after the inception of this book, and to the designers who, without fail, manage to turn my plain words into books which are so beautiful to look at and handle. A debt of gratitude is owed to Jamie Ambrose who corrects my grammar (poor), my spelling (appalling), my inconsistencies (frequent), and my foot-in-the-mouth gaffs (happily rare but horrendous). Thanks again to Janet Betley who is rapidly wearing out the third computer with her endless hours of work, and commiserations to Tony, Louise and Kathi, the family who has probably forgotten what she looks like. Finally, apologies to my wife Sally, who, in our first year of marriage, spent her honeymoon writing the last book and six months being an "author's widow" while I was shut away in the garden shed.

MvS

Superboosters

by Michael van Straten

Superboosters is meant to be used as a general reference and recipe book. While the authors believe the information and recipes it contains are beneficial to health, the book is in no way intended to replace medical advice. You are therefore urged to consult your healthcare professional about specific medical complaints.

First published in Great Britain in 2000 by Mitchell Beazley, an imprint of
Octopus Publishing Group Limited, 2–4 Heron Quays, London E14 4JP
© Octopus Publishing Group Limited 2000
Text © Michael van Straten 2000
Reprinted 2001

A CIP catalogue record for this book is available from the British Library.

This edition produced for The Book People Ltd, Hall Wood Avenue,
Haydock, St Helens WA11 9UL

ISBN 1 84000 561 0

Commissioning Editors: Rebecca Spry, Margaret Little
Executive Art Editors: Tracy Killick, Colin Goody
Design: Miranda Harvey
Managing Editor: Hilary Lumsden
Editor: Jamie Ambrose
Production: Jessame Emms
Index: Ann Barrett

Typeset in Vectora
Printed and bound by Toppan Printing Company in China

contents

introduction

Superboosters may seem a strange title for a book written by a naturopath, which is what I am. Naturopathy is the most holistic of all the complementary therapies, as it not only embraces most of them, but its key principle is to treat the patient, not the symptoms. This book is all about natural supplements that are used specifically to enhance activity, cleanse the system, boost the digestion, heart and circulation, stimulate the immune system, alter moods and increase vitality.

While this may appear to be treating specific symptoms, not people, there are times in everyone's life when a long-term goal of overall health improvement is simply unrealistic. Faced with 24 hours' travel and a vital business dinner with the boss; wedding-night nerves and loss of libido; a key exam after sleepless nights of revision; endless deadlines and not enough hours in the day. . . whatever the particular crisis, what everyone wants, needs and deserves is instant help.

That is what this book is for. *Superboosters* provides safe, natural remedies for many life emergencies of the hectic 21st century. By choosing the remedies in this book, you can avoid the brain-irritating boost of caffeine, the depressive after-effects of alcohol, mind-numbing tranquillizers, a lifetime of Viagra™, antibiotic or handfuls of digestive remedies before and after every meal.

Any medicine strong enough to have an effect will inevitably have a side-effect – even with natural remedies. Yet with most natural medicines, side-effects are mild, nearly always insignificant and transient. Be warned, however: natural can still be deadly. Poisonous mushrooms, deadly nightshade, poison ivy and yew berries are just some of the 'drugs' Nature insists on being treated with respect. And just because St John's wort, echinacea and ginger are all safe individually does not mean that combining them in a super-pill will be equally safe.

The best way to ensure you're taking safe superboosters is to buy standardized products from reputable manufacturers. Do not exceed the recommended dose, do not combine them with prescribed medicines without advice from your doctor or pharmacist and if they produce any adverse reaction, stop using them immediately. The rules are the same for Nature's medicine chest as they are for conventional medicine: use only as directed.

how to use
this book

This book is designed to help you find the most appropriate remedy that will provide the speediest relief for the wide spectrum of conditions covered in each of its chapters. Of course, no universal remedy works as well for every person with the same condition – which is precisely why you will find a choice of easily available supplements from which to choose the best alternative prescription for what ails you or your family. Some of the remedies – guarana, feverfew, valerian, ginseng, artichoke, dandelion, ginger and peppermint – work extremely quickly and can bring rapid relief. Most of the others, however, may take from one to four weeks before their benefits are felt, so don't be impatient and give them a fair try if you want good results. Most of the remedies are available as commercial preparations, but nothing could be simpler than using your own fresh or dried herbs to enhance your health. Follow the easy instructions below and use the quantities stated, unless otherwise directed in individual entries.

Teas

Herbal teas are made by infusing leaves and flowers in boiling water. Special cups with built-in strainers are available in some chemists and health-food stores; alternatively, stir the herb into a cup, or porcelain or glass pot, and strain before use. For one cup, use one teaspoon of dried or two teaspoons of fresh herbs. For a pot, use four teaspoons of dried or two tablespoons of fresh herbs. All teas should be left to stand, covered, for at least ten minutes before drinking; add a little honey to enhance the flavour if desired. Teas can also be kept covered in the refrigerator for 24 hours. Three to four cups daily is the normal dose.

Tinctures

Tinctures are much stronger than teas, can be kept for at least a year and are made by steeping herbs in alcohol. Use 200 grams (7oz) of dried or 300 grams (10½oz) of fresh herb to 1 litre (1¾ pints) of vodka in a large, glass, screw-top jar. Make sure the vodka covers the herbs completely. Keep in a cool, dark place for two weeks, shaking vigorously for a couple of minutes morning and evening. Strain the liquid through a sheet of muslin, then squeeze the leftover material to extract more of the liquid content. Store in a dark, glass bottle and use one teaspoon to half a glass of water, taken two to three times daily.

super
boosters

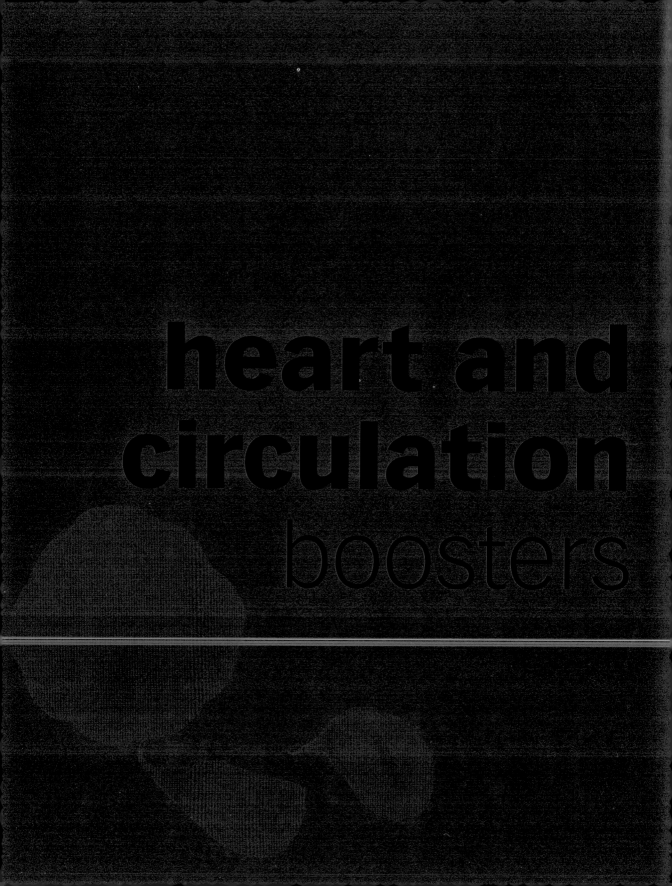

heart and circulation
boosters

Every three minutes in the UK, someone dies from heart disease – the equivalent of a 747 crashing every day of the week and twice on Sundays. What makes these statistics even more tragic is that most of these deaths could have been prevented. Blocked arteries, leaky heart valves, high blood pressure and poor circulation all take their toll in the form of strokes and heart attacks. Smoking, obesity, high cholesterol, lack of exercise, too much booze and a family history of heart disease are all key factors. Having one of these factors on its own is not too serious; have two and you should start worrying. Have three, however, and as they say in baseball, you're out.

The majority of the premature deaths listed above occur in men, yet that balance is changing as more and more women fall prey to the same stresses, lifestyles and bad eating habits that place their male counterparts in hospital. None of the heart and circulatory boosters listed in this chapter will make up for bad diet and lifestyle, but, used appropriately with lifestyle changes, they can play a vital role in improving cardiovascular health.

For example, scientific studies show that folic acid, previously thought to be essential only during early pregnancy, is now a key factor in avoiding heart disease. Garlic helps lower cholesterol levels and blood pressure. Ginkgo biloba opens up the tiniest blood vessels at the extremities of the circulatory system – so it, too, prevents stroke. The potent extracts of the horse chestnut have been used to stimulate circulation since the 17th and 18th centuries. Lycopene, the latest discovery in the protective antioxidants league, joins ranks with selenium, now known to be vital for heart health. The most powerful antioxidant of all, vitamin E, can also help your chances in the heart stakes. Use these superboosters wisely, and with luck, you will never wind up as a statistic.

folic acid
folate

what it is

Folic acid, also known as folate, is part of the vitamin B complex, and it is essential in the formation of DNA: the genetic 'skeleton' of every single cell. A lack of folic acid causes anaemia, and deficiency during the early stages of pregnancy causes genetic abnormalities, specifically spina bifida. Folic acid is found in dark-green vegetables such as broccoli and spinach, in wholemeal bread and wholegrain cereals, in liver, kidneys and nuts. Unfortunately, it is very easily destroyed by overcooking or exposure to bright sunlight.

dosage

In the UK, the recommended daily requirement of folate is 200 micrograms for men and women, plus an extra 100 during pregnancy, and an extra 400 for women planning pregnancy. In America, the levels are 400 micrograms per day for all adults, plus an extra 400 during pregnancy and another 100 when breast-feeding.

precautions

Long-term high dosage of folic acid can mask the symptoms of pernicious anaemia. There are no known adverse reactions with other medications. It is safe during pregnancy and lactation, but only in the recommended doses. Prolonged use of 1,500 micrograms or more a day can lead to abdominal discomfort, appetite loss and the formation of crystals inside the kidney.

what it does

In addition to being essential during **pregnancy**, latest research has shown that low levels of folic acid in the diet lead to increased levels of **homocysteine**, which is a strong predictor of **heart disease**. Some European countries have already legislated to add folic acid to all flour so that their national consumption of this substance is increased. The same legislation is imminent in the UK, and should do much to redress the generally low intake of this **vital nutrient**.

how to use it

In the UK, 400 micrograms daily is advised. Take as a single supplement, as part of a B-complex formula or in a general multi-vitamin and mineral formula. Increase consumption of folate-rich foods. Regular use of antacids or digestive enzyme supplements can interfere with the absorption of folic acid. If using either, an extra dose of 600 micrograms daily is advised.

garlic
allium sativum

what it is

Garlic is the single most versatile, powerful and widely used medicinal plant in the world. A relative of onions, spring onions, leeks and chives, it has an historic use as an anti-fungal and antibacterial, especially effective for the treatment of chest infections. This herb was much loved by the physicians of the ancient world. Slaves building the pyramids were paid in garlic, as were Roman soldiers who brought the bulb to England wedged between their toes to ward off athlete's foot.

Great classical healers such as Hippocrates, Pliny and Diascorides all wrote about garlic and used it for many illnesses. You'll find it in the Bible and ancient Hebrew writings, and the Chinese have used it for 2,500 years. Louis Pasteur also studied it and proved it was a powerful antibacterial in the mid-19th century.

dosage

One medium-sized fresh raw clove per day, or coated tablets of 300mg dried garlic, standardized to produce 1,800 micrograms of allicin; take two daily.

precautions

There are no known interactions with other medications. Skin reactions may occur from handling large quantities of garlic. Mild digestive discomfort has been reported in a few cases. Because it thins the blood, do not take garlic supplements two or three weeks before undergoing surgery; tell your doctor if you have been using them. Garlic is considered safe to take during pregnancy or breast-feeding.

what it does

In the 1980s, research began to demonstrate the amazing value of garlic in the **protection** of the **heart** and **circulatory system**. Several hundred published research papers show that garlic can lower **cholesterol,** reduce **blood pressure** and make the blood less sticky, thus reducing the risk of clots. A regular intake of garlic not only protects the heart and circulation and boosts their function, but also protects against food poisoning, other bacterial and fungal infections and even has some **cancer-fighting** properties.

Sulphur-rich compounds released when garlic is crushed not only produce its characteristic smell but also most of its **therapeutic** benefits. For this reason, supplements that are deodorized or made solely of extracted garlic oil are not as effective as either the whole bulb or the standardized whole extract.

how to use it

If you can't bear the taste, take garlic as tablets, but everyone would benefit from one fresh clove a day (or standardized tablets providing an equivalent dose).

what it is

Ginkgo biloba, also known as the maidenhair tree, is the most ancient and one of the longest-surviving plants on earth. Individual trees can live up to 1,000 years, and its medicinal use is recorded 5,000 years ago in Chinese traditional medicine. The tree's leaves are used medicinally. Gentle drying ensures that only the water is removed, then the whole leaf is crushed and made into tablets, which are standardized to ensure an accurate daily intake of its active ingredients.

ginkgo biloba
the maidenhair tree

available as

Capsules
Tablets
Tea bags

dosage

Up to 220mg daily of standardized ginkgo biloba extract, providing 60mg active ginkgo flavonglycosides and 14.4mg ginkgolides and bilobalide.

precautions

There are no reports of interactions with other medications, and no contra-indications for use during pregnancy or breast-feeding. Very rarely, people have reported mild headaches or stomach upsets for the first day or two of taking the tablets. These symptoms then fade.

what it does

The potent natural chemicals in ginkgo extract have the unique ability to improve **circulation** to the brain, at the same time reducing the stickiness of the blood. Research shows that ginkgo is highly effective in improving **short-term memory** loss in the elderly. Even people in the early stages of **Alzheimer's** disease can benefit from ginkgo biloba. There is no evidence that the plant is in any way a treatment for Alzheimer's, but given in the early stages of the illness it appears to delay the worsening of symptoms by many months.

Research conducted by Professor Ian Hindmarch, of the Human Psychopharamacology Research Unit at the University of Surrey, surveyed the impact of ginkgo on a group of volunteers who were young, healthy and had no memory problems. The results demonstrated that ginkgo improved **concentration**, psycho-motor skills and memory in the group taking 120mg of extract daily.

As a general **circulatory stimulant**, ginkgo is helpful in the treatment of **Raynaud's disease**, chilblains and tinnitus.

how to use it

Take as a standardized extract, high-dose 120mg tablets, two together with breakfast. Alternatively, take three tablets daily containing 50mg ginkgo extract at meal times.

what it is

The horse chestnut is a large, deciduous tree boasting 'candles' of beautiful pink and white flowers, and rough-covered seeds – the horse chestnuts themselves. Left to their own devices, the trees can grow to a huge 24.4 metres (80+ ft), with a massive canopy that provides a cooling haven on hot summer days.

Originating in eastern Europe and Asia, the horse chestnut now grows in most temperate climatic zones. Known as a medicinal plant since Roman times, extracts of the seeds were more commonly used throughout Europe than in the UK. In the past, the bark, chestnuts and leaves have all been used, but modern preparations consist of standardized extracts taken from the seeds, which have the richest concentration of active substances.

horse chestnut
aesculus hippocastanum

available as
Dried seed
Gel
Tablets

dosage
0.5 to 1 gram of dried seed. Standardized extract: 15 to 20 per cent aescin content, providing 50 to 100mg of aescin daily, reducing to 25 to 50mg for maintenance.

precautions

Use only standardized extracts with known aescin content; do not exceed recommended doses. Do not take or use topically if suffering from kidney or liver disease, if pregnant or breast-feeding, and do not use for children under 14. Rarely, horse chestnut may cause local allergic reactions when applied topically. There are no reports of interactions with other medications.

what it does

Although traditionally horse chestnut was utilized for its **cleansing** and **anti-inflammatory** properties, its most important use is in the treatment of peripheral **circulatory disorders**. Aescin, the most powerful of its constituents, acts specifically as a **tonic** to vein walls, making this an excellent remedy for the relief of **varicose veins**, fluid retention and piles. Local application is excellent for reducing **swelling** after an injury.

how to use it

As a standardized extract of dried seeds. Use as a gel applied to painful regions morning and evening.

lycopene

what it is

When Christopher Columbus brought tomatoes back from South America to Europe in 1498, little did he know how important this delicious fruit would become. During the final years of the 20th century, scientists discovered that eating tomatoes, tomato sauce, tomato paste and ketchup can help prevent heart disease. The reason? The protective antioxidant known as lycopene, the richest source of which is indeed the tomato. The human body cannot manufacture its own lycopene, nor does it convert lycopene into vitamin A, as it does with other carotenoids. All the lycopene we need must come from food. Researchers have found far less of this heart-saving substance in the fat of men who have had heart attacks than in the fat of those who have not.

dosage

Eat lots of vine-ripened tomatoes and tomato products, or take one 10mg capsule daily.

precautions

There are no reported interactions with other medications. There is no contra-indication for taking lycopene during pregnancy or breast-feeding.

what it does

According to Dr Venket Rao, from the Department of Nutritional Sciences at the University of Toronto, Canada, "Population studies have recently shown that women consuming high levels of tomatoes and tomato products rich in lycopene are less likely to suffer from breast, ovarian and cervical **cancers**. These are the most common cancers in women and the principal cause of cancer-related deaths.

Although lycopene is similar to other carotenoids such as beta-carotene, the unique way in which it works together with vitamin C makes it a most powerful **protective** antioxidant. Professor Truscott from Keele University, UK, speculates that lycopene may slow the onset of age-related macular degeneration (AMD), the most common cause of poor vision and eventually **blindness**, in the elderly.

Numerous studies show that those eating more tomatoes or having more lycopene in their blood have significantly lower rates of cancer. The best protection is against cancers of the prostate, **lung and stomach,** but the **pancreas**, colon, rectum, oesophagus, mouth, **breast** and cervix are also protected.

how to use it

Consume fresh tomatoes and tomato products such as purée, paste and ketchup on a regular basis. If you are allergic to tomatoes (or not a fan of them or their by-products), take a daily lycopene supplement.

selenium

what it is

Selenium is an essential mineral that is worryingly deficient in the average UK diet. The minimum daily requirement for adult males is 75 micrograms per day; for females, 60 micrograms per day. The daily amount provided by food has declined by 50 per cent over the last 20 years to an average of 35 micrograms per day for men and women. We used to get most of our selenium from bread made with North American and Canadian wheat. The wheat grew on selenium-rich soil; consequently, it contained substantial amounts. Since the advent of the Common Market, we no longer import these grains, and make do with European wheats containing much less selenium. Other good food sources are Brazil nuts, wholegrain foods, onions, garlic, sesame seeds and shellfish.

Selenium first came to international prominence through American involvement with China and 'Keshan Disease'. This condition produced a vast rate of heart disease in young men in the Keshan province, where the soil is almost devoid of selenium. An American drug company provided selenium supplements; halfway through a double-blind trial, it was so obvious which group was getting the real pill that the study was abandoned – and selenium supplements were given to all participants.

dosage

Up to 200 micrograms daily.

precautions

There are no reports of interactions with other medicines. It is safe to take selenium during pregnancy and breast-feeding, but only at the recommended dose. Long-term use of 1,000 micrograms a day or more can have serious side-effects, such as rashes or damage to the nervous system.

what it does

Selenium is the **essential link** in the activation of an **antioxidant** enzyme called glutathione peroxidase. Without sufficient selenium, the enzyme cannot do its job as a **heart-protector** and **cancer-preventer**. Selenium is also essential for normal **thyroid function**. A large number of studies show that an abundant intake of selenium reduces the risk of fatty deposits in the arteries and damage to the **heart muscle**, as well as the risk of breast and **prostate** cancers.

how to use it

A daily supplement is one of the most important superboosters to add to your normal regime. Selenium is normally combined with yeast for better absorption. For all-round heart and circulatory benefits, it is best taken in combination with vitamins A, C and E.

vitamin e

what it is

Vitamin E is one of the most essential of all the protective antioxidants. It is vital for the good health and proper functioning of the heart and circulatory system. Although vitamin E was discovered almost 60 years ago, new research continues to produce exciting results. In the US, scientists studied a group of 87,000 female nurses and 40,000 male health workers for eight years; those taking a daily supplement of vitamin E – at least 100 international units (IU) – showed a 40 per cent reduction in the risk of heart disease.

In the UK, the Cambridge Heart Antioxidant Study (CHAOS), a European multi-centre study in which the volunteers were given between 400 and 800 IU of vitamin E each day, showed a resulting reduction of 75 per cent in the occurrence of non-fatal heart attacks.

dosage

200 to 400 IU daily. Up to
10,000 IU with professional advice.

precautions

There are no reported interactions
with other medications, and no
evidence of contra-indication during
pregnancy or breast-feeding. If your
diet contains large amounts of
polyunsaturated fats, you will need
to increase your intake of vitamin E.

what it does

Vitamin E **protects** the actual membrane of every individual **cell** in
the body, and that includes protecting fat-soluble tissues such as LDL:
the dangerous type of cholesterol. It is generally believed that only
damaged LDL cells have the ability to cause arterial and heart
problems; by protecting the cholesterol cells, vitamin E also protects
the **heart** and **blood vessels**.

The list of benefits covers virtually all **inflammatory** conditions,
but the certain advantages of consuming extra vitamin E come from
its **cardiovascular** activity. It is also useful in the treatment of osteo-
and rheumatoid arthritis, **eczema**, infertility and the menopause.

how to use it

Take in capsules, but also
ensure a good dietary
intake from wheatgerm
and olive oils, nuts, seeds,
eggs, dark-green leafy
vegetables and avocados.

protective
boosters

The old adage that 'we must eat a peck of dirt before we die' has far more than a grain of truth in it. Exposing the immune system to the occasional 'pecks of dirt', bacteria and viruses kick-starts it into action, so that it comes leaping to our defence when we need it most. The modern obsession with excessive hygiene deprives many children's immune systems of the daily challenges they have been biologically designed to meet. Antiseptic sprays for every surface; disinfectants for all nooks and crannies; food devoid of natural bacteria abound in most modern homes. Yet this is only half of the story. The creeping tentacles of the factory-farming industry reach into every household. Poultry, eggs, meat, milk, cheese, butter, cream and yoghurt are all likely to carry traces of antibiotics used (legally and illegally) during production; these pass into the food chain and then into us and our children.

This continuous drip-feed and the over-prescription of antibiotics in recent years encourage the development of resistant strains of bacteria. The result? Neither the body's own defences nor existing antibiotic medicines are effective against these invaders. Pollution, ozone and carbon particulates given off by office machines and nutrient-deficient diets only make matters worse. In the end, all that is needed are a few stressful days, an opportunistic bacteria or virus – and disaster strikes.

Fortunately, Nature is full of potent plants that can reinvigorate your natural defence system. Cat's claw, for example, can improve immunity by 50 per cent. The cranberry boosts resistance to urinary infections, while the Australian tea tree prevents infection. All these and more are available to help fend off illness: some as long-term protectors, others as immune boosters when infection strikes. By using these safe and effective natural defenders, you can reserve your use of pharmaceuticals for the times when you really need them.

cat's claw
uncaria tomentosa

what it is

Cat's claw is a vine that grows high into the canopy roof of the Amazonian rain forest, and gets its name from the claw-like thorns which protrude from its woody stems. Besides its native Amazon, it is also found in tropical regions of Peru, Colombia, Ecuador and other parts of South America.

Cat's claw is popular with many Peruvian tribes, who are known to have used it for at least 2,000 years, yet it was virtually unheard of in the rest of the world until the 1970s. At that time, stories began appearing in the press about its use as a cancer medicine, and the fame of this traditional remedy spread worldwide almost overnight. Traditionally, the plant has been used as an anti-inflammatory, for wound healing and as a treatment for rheumatism, ulcers and dysentery; in addition, early research into its cancer-fighting properties has shown promise. In 1993, however, scientists found that cat's claw could also boost the immune system of patients with HIV.

dosage

Up to 60 mg of standardized extract daily or 1,000 mg whole dried plant.

precautions

There are no reported interactions with other medications, and no serious adverse effects have been noted. However, avoid during pregnancy and breast-feeding.

what it does

Cat's claw is one of nature's great **immune boosters**. It contains some very important chemicals called oxyindole alkaloids, which have a specific effect of **stimulating** the immune system. Only small amounts of these alkaloids are necessary to boost immunity by around 50 per cent; other studies have shown **tumour-** and **leukaemia-fighting** benefits, too. The overall immune-boosting benefits of cat's claw make this rain forest plant an excellent choice as a **protector** and general help-mate for the body's **natural defence** mechanisms. As yet, there is no definitive evidence of its benefits in the treatment of **HIV**, AIDS or cancer, but it is certainly worth trying as an adjunct to conventional therapy.

how to use it

Make tea by boiling 1 gram of root bark in a cup of water for ten minutes; cool, strain and drink a cup three times daily. Alternatively, certified tea bags deliver an infusion equal to 1,500 to 1,800 mg of plant extract. The herb is also available in capsules of 500 or 1,000 mg.

cranberry
vaccinium macrocarpon

what it is

Cranberries are native to North America. For centuries, Native Americans used these extraordinary berries as both food and medicine. They bathed their wounds in cranberry juice, and their medicine men made cranberry poultices to draw out the poison from arrow injuries. Ever since the North American Indians discovered the health-giving benefits of cranberries, they have become a favourite medicinal fruit of traditional herbalists and naturopaths. In recent years, science has unravelled some of the mysteries of this extraordinary bog plant and confirmed its traditional value. Most women know about cranberry juice and cystitis, but the latest research shows that the berries may protect against breast cancer, too.

dosage

100 to 300mg of standardized cranberry extract per day.

precautions

There are no known interactions with other medications and no reported side-effects. Cranberries and cranberry juice are safe to take during pregnancy and breast-feeding.

what it does

Traditionally, it was thought that the acidity of cranberry juice produced its **anti-bacterial** effect. However, between 1984 and 1986, when Dr Anthony Sobota, Professor of Microbiology at Youngstown State University, Ohio, published the results of his research, the true explanation began to emerge. Cranberries contain a component that covers the walls of the bladder, **kidneys** and interconnecting tubing; this substance **prevents** bacteria from attaching to these sensitive tissues, where they would normally live and multiply. Sobota found that a glass of supermarket cranberry juice a day was ten times as **effective** at killing urinary bacteria as conventional antibiotics.

A follow-up study, published in March 1994 by doctors Gerry Avorn, Mark Monane, Gerry Gurwitz and others of the Harvard University Medical School reported the findings of the first placebo-controlled, large-scale clinical trial to test the effects of cranberry juice. Within a month of beginning the trial, **positive** results appeared in the majority of patients drinking the real cranberry juice. Other research has shown that the most chronic sufferers stay **infection-free** as long as they drink their one glass of cranberry juice a day.

how to use it

Drink at least one pint a day of a 50/50 dilution of cranberry juice with water, both as a treatment during an attack of cystitis and for long-term protection against it. Cranberry extract is also available in tablet and capsule form.

what it is

Another Native American herbal remedy, echinacea has become an important natural medicine throughout the world. Although it is still often harvested from the wild, most commercial preparations come from farmed crops of the plant. Both the leaf and root have medicinal properties.

The American Indians traditionally used it on cuts, burns and other injuries to prevent infection, and the Sioux and Comanche tribes revered the plant for its healing properties. Historically it has been used for a wide range of conditions including allergies, asthma and chilblains, but most modern research has studied its value as a natural, safe immune-booster.

echinacea
echinacea angustifolia

available as

Capsules
Tablets
Tincture

dosage

Half a teaspoon of tincture in water three times a day. Capsules of 300mg powdered root and leaf, plus 125mg standardized extract: one, three times daily.

precautions

There are no reported adverse reactions with other medications. Echinacea appears safe to take during pregnancy and breast-feeding. However, do not take continuously for ongoing protection, as this may reduce the strength of your natural immunity.

what it does

A century and a half ago, echinacea first appeared in the United States Dispensatory and was listed as a medicine that increased **resistance** to infection. Physiologically, it **stimulates** the production of white blood cells for protection against bacteria, and helps the body produce more **interferon** for increased protection against viruses. Its main constituents are polysaccharides, betaine, alkalides and echinolone. The combination of these natural chemicals is the key to the plant's **immune-boosting** success, which also extends to protection against **fungal infections**. Echinacea is a great gargle for sore throats, and can be extremely helpful in the treatment of chronic **viral conditions** such as ME.

how to use it

Take standardized extract, capsules or tinctures at the first sign of any infectious illness. If colleagues or family catch colds, then take echinacea before you get sick – but not for more than two or three weeks.

what it is

Of all the herbs used by the ancient Incas, lapacho was one of the mainstays. In the four centuries since the Spanish Conquest, the herb has cropped up from time to time in Europe. Czar Nicholas II and Ghandi are both known to have done what millions of Brazilians do: start their day with a cup of lapacho tea.

Also called pau d'arco, ipe roxo or taheebo, lapacho is a rain forest medicine made from the inner bark of the large native South American tree known as tabebuia. Throughout South America, indigenous tribes have drunk tea made from the shredded inner bark to boost the effectiveness of the body's own immune defence mechanisms. They have also used this traditional remedy for centuries in the treatment of asthma, bronchitis, infection and also some forms of cancer.

As far back as 1882, one of lapacho's constituents was isolated and identified as lapachol, an anti-microbial and potentially tumour-fighting chemical. Today, scientific evidence shows that crude extracts of lapachol – more potent than refined versions – offer effective protection against a wide range of bacterial and fungal organisms, including *Candida albicans*, which causes thrush.

lapacho
tabebuia impestiginosa
pau d'arco

available as

Capsules
Dried bark

dosage

2 to 5 grams of
powdered bark daily.

precautions

Using whole bark has no known serious side-effects, nor are there reported interactions with other medicines. However, this herb is not suitable during pregnancy or lactation. Care should be taken if using concentrated extracts, as overdosing can cause vomiting, nausea and bleeding.

what it does

Rain forest Indians have always valued lapacho as a **powerful** medicine for **strengthening** immunity and to **protect** them against gut parasites. Research at São Paulo, Harvard, the University of Munich, the University of Rio de Janeiro and the American National Cancer Institute has increased awareness of this amazing natural medicine. In many parts of the world, physicians are recognizing it as an aid to patients with **immune-deficiency** illnesses.

For ME, **chronic fatigue syndrome**, Epstein-Barr and Tired All The Time Syndrome, lapacho can be a great aid to **recovery** due to its positive effects on the immune system.

how to use it

As capsules of finely ground bark powder, usually 500 mg in each. These should be taken at a dose of two to three capsules three times daily.

lemon balm
melissa officinalis

what it is

Lemon balm is a perennial herb growing up to 1½ metres (5ft) in height, with a mass of tiny white flowers. Although it originated in the Mediterranean and central Europe, it is now common throughout America and has escaped from English gardens to spread throughout the countryside. The ancient Greeks dedicated this herb to the goddess Diana and named it *Melissa* – meaning 'bee'. More than 2,000 years ago, they observed that bees adored the fragrant white flowers and were attracted by the pollen.

To this day, clever gardeners plant lemon balm around their orchards to encourage pollination, and beekeepers use it to keep their swarms close to home. The main constituents of lemon balm are volatile oils, flavonoids and polyphenols, which endow the plant with such an extraordinary range of benefits.

dosage

Tea: two to three cups daily. Tincture: half a teaspoon in water three times a day. Essential oil: five drops to a teaspoon of grape seed oil for local application.

precautions

There are no reports of serious adverse reactions, or of interaction with other medications. Lemon balm is safe to take when driving, also with modest amounts of alcohol. Lemon balm tea or tincture are safe when pregnant or breast-feeding. Some reports indicate that lemon balm essential oil may have an adverse effect on anyone suffering from glaucoma, as it has been shown to raise the pressure in the eye.

what it does

The ancient Greeks used lemon balm to improve the **memory**, relieve **headaches** and overcome **depression**. From the Middle Ages onwards, it has been a popular remedy for tension, headaches, toothache, skin conditions and depression.

While these effects are a factual matter of observation, the most exciting modern use of lemon balm is as an **anti-viral**. Local applications of essential oil can shorten the duration of an attack of *Herpes simplex* (the **cold sore** virus) by several days. At the very first sign of prickling and tingling in the lips, apply the oil several times daily and drink two to three cups of lemon balm tea.

Regular use of this delicious **aromatic** herb in salads and cooking will certainly strengthen the immune system and protect specifically against viral infections. It can also be valuable in the treatment of **neuralgic** pain and indigestion.

how to use it

Use as tea – one heaped tablespoon of fresh leaves to a cup of boiling water – tincture or essential oil. Use fresh leaves in salads and cooking.

tea tree
melaleuca alternifolia

what it is

Tea tree, a relative of the myrtle, is a modest evergreen tree that grows to about 7.3 metres (24ft). Native to Australia, it is one of the most important local medicines used by the Aborigines. Their knowledge of its powerful healing properties has been passed from generation to generation for thousands of years. They used it by pounding the leaves and placing them on the affected area like a poultice, or by bathing in pools over which tea trees grew. It was Captain Cook who gave the tree its name, as he and his crew used the leaves as a substitute for Indian or China tea.

dosage

For topical application: five drops of essential oil to 15 ml of grape seed oil, or any other available pure vegetable oil; or add five drops to one teaspoon of any moisturising cream. For internal use: half a teaspoon of infusion to a cup of warm water twice daily.

precautions

Do not apply neat tea tree oil to broken skin or to rashes, near eyes, nose, mouth or genital regions. When using tea tree oil for the first time, test on a small sensitive area of skin, such as the inside of the forearm, and wait 24 hours before using it on larger areas. There are no reports of adverse reactions with other medications. Tea tree oil is safe for external use during pregnancy and breast-feeding, but avoid internal mixtures.

what it does

Tea tree is powerfully **antiseptic**, **anti-fungal** and **anti-bacterial**, and has the effect of giving your immune system a shot in the arm. The action of the plant's natural terpenoids accounts for these properties; the most important of them is terpinen-4-ol. This **potent** substance is a very important antiseptic that is also non-irritating to most skin types. Scientific evidence of tea tree's remarkable powers has abounded in Australia since the 1920s, and products made from it have proliferated in the UK during the past ten years. Good-quality organic tea tree oil is a **pure**, **safe** substance that deserves a place in every home's medicine chest. It is now available commercially in shampoos, lotions, creams, talcum powder and even as a foot spray for the treatment of **athlete's foot**.

how to use it

A few drops of essential oil in a bowl of hot water releases decongestant steam for the nose and throat. Six or seven drops in the bath helps prevent thrush and other fungal diseases. Two or three cups of tea tree tea made from a teaspoon of dried leaves or half a teaspoon of tincture to a cup of warm water increase resistance to bacterial, viral and fungal attacks.

turmeric
curcuma longa

what it is

Turmeric is a member of the ginger family and is native to India and China. It grows to a height of approximately 1 metre (3ft) and is cultivated for the medicinal value of its root, which is most commonly used as a flavouring and yellow colourant in Chinese and other Far Eastern cooking.

Turmeric is available in both fresh and dried forms. This essential ingredient of curry powder is also widely used in southern Asian cooking. It is a key to successful Asian vegetarian food and is thought particularly important in the preparation of lentils. The most valuable of the plant's chemicals are its volatile oils, particularly curcumin, which is extracted and sold as a specific medicinal substance.

dosage

Up to 1.5 grams a day of curcumin extracted from turmeric, or one teaspoon of dried turmeric powder to a cup of water three times daily.

precautions

There are no reports of adverse reactions or interactions with other drugs. Using turmeric as a culinary spice is safe during pregnancy and breast-feeding. However, there is no data available on large doses of curcumin in respect of pregnancy, so it is probably best avoided.

what it does

Prescribed for centuries by Ayurvedic practitioners in India, turmeric was used in the treatment of bad **eyesight**, **rheumatism**, arthritis and **liver problems**. As well as confirming the traditional activities of turmeric, scientists are now fascinated by its powerful **antioxidant** and **protective** properties, which appear to work in a similar way to the latest non-steroidal **anti-inflammatories**, the Cox-2 inhibitors. But turmeric has one huge advantage: there are no side-effects.

how to use it

Incorporate turmeric in cooking to make it a regular part of your daily diet. For emergency situations, when your resistance is low or bacterial and viral infections are rampant, take capsules of curcumin for a two- to three-week period.

mood
boosters

In this 21st century, we may think we are more subject to stress than at any other time in man's history. Mobile phones, urgent e-mails, deadlines, job insecurity, mortgages, divorce, difficult children, the apparent breakdown of family life and reports of ever-increasing crime and violence all serve to make us less than relaxed. It isn't surprising that so many people seek solace through drugs (legal and otherwise), alcohol and other mind-affecting substances – yet there is nothing new about seeking the ability to alter moods.

Some of man's earliest experiments with plants originated in the quest for mood enhancement – mainly because our forefathers endured different but equally mood-disrupting circumstances on a daily basis. They faced starvation, marauding animals and aggressive neighbouring tribes, with little or no help to cope with injury, pain, disease and death. When times were bad, they found comfort in plants that helped them feel good. The Pacific islanders, for example, discovered that kava kava reduced anxiety and induced happiness, while natives of both North and South America used the beautiful passion-flower to cope with stress. The ancient Greeks used St John's wort to relieve depression, while the medicine men of European tribes knew the value of feverfew, not just for migraines but for the relief of mental exhaustion that follows an attack. More recently, science has isolated phosphatidylserine, a chemical that improves mental function, lifts depression and may help in treating Alzheimer's Disease.

Of course, powerful mind-altering drugs are needed to treat serious mental disorders. Yet using a chemical straight-jacket of tranquillizers, anti-depressants and stimulants for the ups and downs of everyday life or occasional bouts of mild depression has to be the ultimate madness. Why not let the super mood-boosters in this chapter take the strain? They work – in most cases – without side-effects.

black cohosh
cimicifuga racemosa

what it is

Black cohosh is yet another of the Native American medicines that started life in the eastern regions of America and Canada. It now grows wild in Europe, too, as a garden escapee. An herbaceous perennial, black cohosh is a relative of the buttercup, and grows to about 2.4 metres (8 ft) in height, with attractive spikes of cream flowers. The plant was named *cohosh* by the Algonquin Indians; the word means 'rough', which is an apt description of its dark, twisted root.

Fortunately, those natives weren't put off by the unpleasant smell and bitter flavour of this herb, which they used to great effect in the relief of rheumatic pain, joint disorders as well as more traditionally in problems of the menstrual cycle. The key constituents are triterpene glycosides and a group of isoflavones, which are hormone-like substances. Salicylic acid and isoferulic acid are also present, and the combined pain-reducing and oestrogen-like effects are the result of the herb's complex chemical construction.

dosage

Standardized extracts as tincture or tablets, 250mg providing 40 to 50mg of extract or up to 2 grams a day of dried root.

precautions

There are no reported interactions with other medications. Not suitable for pregnant or breast-feeding women. Women should seek medical advice if using oestrogen-based medication. Large doses can cause headaches, nausea and dizziness, among other side effects. Not advised for children, or in large doses for the elderly. Avoid long-term use.

what it does

The traditional use of black cohosh is for the **relief** of the physical and psychological symptoms of the menstrual cycle and the **menopause**. It is particularly effective in the relief of hot flushes and general malaise of menopause, and helps lift the **low mood** that often accompanies unpleasant menopausal symptoms.

Black cohosh is also a valuable **anti-inflammatory**, and inhibits the production of progesterone from the ovaries by decreasing the levels of stimulated hormones. The general **sedative effects** of the plant may also be helpful in the relief of **tinnitus**.

how to use it

The most convenient way to take black cohosh is in tablet form as a standardized concentrated extract. Tablets are usually equivalent to 40 to 50mg of the fresh herb. Up to 2 grams a day of the dried root or 500mg powdered extract or half a teaspoon of tincture are normal daily doses.

feverfew
tanacetum parthenium

what it is

Feverfew is an attractive member of the chrysanthemum family, and it was originally native to parts of southern Europe. Today, however, it has spread all over Europe, the UK and North America. This useful perennial grows to a height of about 0.6 metres (2 ft) and has masses of attractive yellow and white flowers that resemble daisies. Gardeners beware: it is highly invasive.

Although feverfew was used traditionally in the treatment of all types of fevers it was the 17th-century English herbalist Nicholas Culpeper who first recommended it for headaches; he also maintained that it was one of the best of all herbs for women. In modern times, this herb has become synonymous with the relief of migraines, an action attributed to the phytochemical (plant chemical) parthenolide. The plant also contains valuable volatile oils and camphor. While a wide range of manufactured feverfew products are on the market, it is easy to grow and use and deserves a place in everyone's garden – migraine sufferer or not.

dosage

Two to three fresh leaves daily.
Up to 1.5 grams of dried leaf powder
daily. As a tincture, add five drops
to a glass of water and take
three times daily.

precautions

Eating the fresh leaf may cause
mouth ulcers. Not advised during
pregnancy or breast-feeding; not
for children under 12. Do not
take feverfew if you have been
prescribed aspirin, warfarin or
other blood-thinning drugs, as it
may reduce the effectiveness of
your medication. Rarely, some
people may develop skin
sensitivity to the leaves.

what it does

Feverfew appears to have a powerful **anti-inflammatory** action,
which would explain its historical use in the treatment of rheumatism
and **arthritis**. Roman physicians found it valuable in treating
menstrual problems and used it as an aid to stimulate the start of
periods. Although feverfew had been used as an effective treatment for
migraine and headaches for more than 300 years, it wasn't until the
1970s that any serious clinical evaluation was undertaken. The results
confirmed the wisdom of 17th-century herbalists and showed that
around 70 per cent of migraine sufferers could **benefit** to a greater
or lesser degree from this simple, safe and very inexpensive remedy.
Exactly how feverfew works is still something of a mystery, yet it
appears that the parthenolide **reduces** the amount of the hormone
serotonin. **Serotonin**, which is produced by the body, is thought to
be a likely trigger of migraine attacks.

how to use it

Eat two to three leaves
a day; for many migraine
sufferers, this is enough to
prevent recurrent attacks.
It is important to put the
leaves into a sandwich,
as eaten alone, they can
cause severe and
unpleasant mouth ulcers.
Feverfew is also available
as standardized tablets
and as capsules of dried
powdered leaf.

what it is

This large climbing shrub is a native Polynesian vine that is found all over the Pacific islands. It has been used since the earliest times to make a mind-altering liquid that played an essential part in both social and religious ceremonies. The root of kava kava is transformed into a non-alcoholic drink by the Pacific islanders. Its use as a modern herbal remedy is based on its traditional mood-enhancing benefits, including a long-standing and justified reputation as an aphrodisiac. This valuable member of the pepper family contains a unique resin made up of kava lactones, as well as the alkaloid pipermethysticine.

kava kava
piper methysticum

available as
Capsules

dosage
Up to 200mg of kava lactones per day.

precautions

Do not take continuously for more than three months. Excessive doses lead to euphoria and the appearance of drunkenness. Not suitable during pregnancy or breast-feeding. Do not take with alcohol or prescribed mind-affecting medication. Not suitable in the treatment of severe depression.

what it does

In modest doses, kava kava is best known as a **safe** treatment for stress and **anxiety**. Unlike many prescribed tranquillizers, the herb does not cause drowsiness or interfere with the ability to drive or operate dangerous machinery in safety. It is a remarkable remedy for overcoming the problems of extended periods of **stress** and anxiety, and it also helps relieve the **muscle tension** and subsequent pain that often accompanies unrelieved emotional stress.

Some scientific studies have revealed that kava kava is as good a tranquillizer as the benzodiazepines, but without their addictive problems. Kava kava is also helpful in relieving the pain of osteo- and **rheumatoid arthritis**, as well as other forms of chronic and intractable **pain**.

how to use it

Best taken as a standardized preparation of root extract combined with root powder in the form of capsules.

what it is

This popular climbing vine, adorned with beautiful purple flowers, can grow to around 9 metres (30 ft) in length. Although indigenous to South, Central and North America, varieties of this vigorous plant now grow almost everywhere. Its delicious fruit seldom develops in the UK or northern Europe, though it may do so during a long, hot summer.

Passion-flower has been popular with European herbalists since the late 1500s, and its virtues as a tranquillizing herb have been praised in herbal textbooks since that time. In North America, the herb has been widely used and studied for at least 150 years. A traditional treatment for anxiety and insomnia – and applied locally for headaches and injuries – it has an ancient history among the Aztecs, Amazonian Indians and native North Americans. The plant acquired its name from 16th-century Spanish missionaries, who believed the flower represented the crucifixion: the three styles for the nails through Christ's hands and feet, and the five stamens for His wounds.

passion-flower
passiflora incarnata
maracuja

available as
Capsules
Tablets
Tincture

dosage
6 grams of dried herb as an infusion (made as tea) daily.

precautions

There are no reported side-effects or interactions with other medications. Some experts suggest that it should not be taken with the MAOI category of anti-depressants. Passion-flower is safe for children. There are no known reports of harmful effects during pregnancy or breast-feeding.

what it does

The most important constituents are **flavonoids**, especially apigenin and isovitexin and the glycosides, including gynocardin. The flowers, leaves and stems are used fresh or dried for their **calming** effects. Passion-flower is extremely **valuable** for the treatment of **insomnia**, agitation, irritability and anxiety. Less well-researched, though high on the list of traditional uses, are its **anti-spasmodic** qualities: it may be safely used for **stomach cramp**, palpitations, high blood pressure and colic.

how to use it

Passion-flower can be taken as a tea, tincture or as commercially available tablets or extracts. It is often found combined with lemon balm, valerian or other mood-enhancing herbs.

phosphatidylserine

what it is

Phosphatidylserine (PS) is one of a special group of essential nutrients known as phospholipids. These substances are vital for the proper structure of the cell membranes, and PS is particularly abundant in brain cells. Only tiny traces are found in food, and the body manufactures its own from other phospholipids. Its main function is in the transmission of electrical impulses from cell to cell, and of all the phospholipids, PS has the most dramatic effects on brain function when used as a nutritional supplement.

Commercially available PS is a concentrated form of phosphatidylserine made by a special process that enables it to be extracted from the phospholipids in soya beans. This natural plant form of PS is readily available, as it is well absorbed by the body. It is ideal to take by mouth.

dosage

Up to 300 mg per day.

precautions

There are no reported adverse side-effects or interactions with prescribed medications.

what it does

This naturally occurring 'good fat' is particularly abundant in brain cells, where it plays a key role in regulating the function of the **brain**. Unfortunately for many people otherwise in good health, some mental ability starts to decline with age. As early as the middle 40s, parts of the brain that govern **memory**, learning and **concentration** can lose up to half their working capacity. This is where PS can come to the rescue.

Extensive research has demonstrated repeatedly how this **safe** supplement works as a powerful **mood booster**. PS can improve brain function dramatically in the over-50s, and virtually all adults over the age of 45 are likely to benefit from small but regular doses. One of the most remarkable studies examined 150 people between the ages of 50 and 75 who were all having difficulty with remembering phone numbers, misplacing things, poor concentration and inability to memorize even short pieces of text. After a month of daily PS, the symptoms improved so much that it was as if their **mental clocks** had been turned back by 12 years.

how to use it

Initially, 200 to 300 mg a day should be taken for one month, then as symptoms improve, reduce to 200 mg, then 100 mg daily. If medication is ceased completely, memory, concentration and cognitive functions will start to decline, so I recommend a continual maintenance regime of 100 mg a day every third week.

phosphatidylserine **55**

st john's wort
hypericum perforatum

what it is

An upright perennial growing to around 1 metre (3ft) high with attractive brilliant-yellow flowers, St John's wort grows wild throughout Europe. It flowers normally around St John's Day, June 24th, which is how it gets its common name.

For centuries, St John's wort been used in the treatment of chest infections, bladder problems, for wound healing, and as a gentle sedative. Its modern use, however, is mainly for the treatment of mild to moderate depression; over two million people have tried it for this reason in the UK alone. Even this is not a new treatment: the ancient Greeks called St John's wort the 'sunshine herb', as it brought light back into the lives of depressed people.

dosage

400 to 600mg of dried extract, equivalent to 900 micrograms total hypericin daily.

precautions

There is evidence of interaction with some prescribed medicines, specifically the blood-thinning drug warfarin. It could also interfere with drugs for HIV, organ transplants and epilepsy, with theophiline for asthma, some anti-depressants, triptans for migraine and low-dose contraceptive pills. Best avoided during pregnancy and breast-feeding

what it does

St John's wort contains volatile oil, **flavonoids** and, most importantly, hypericin, which is not only **anti-depressant** but also has powerful anti-viral properties. Hypericin is found in all parts of the plant. A recent analysis of 23 different clinical trials has shown beyond doubt that St John's wort is extremely effective in the **relief** of mild to moderate depression. Yet even mild depression can trigger a range of distressing symptoms: insomnia, **exhaustion**, tiredness, muscle pain, headaches and palpitations – symptoms that can all be helped by St John's wort. Repeated double-blind studies have proved that individuals suffering from mild to moderate depression respond as well to this gentle and **non-addictive** herb as they do to more powerful chemical sedatives, tranquillizers and anti-depressants.

Despite some suggestions of interactions with other medications (see 'precautions'), I believe that St John's wort is infinitely **safer** than aspirin, paracetamol or other anti-inflammatory drugs. To put it another way, 87 million St John's wort tablets were manufactured by the Kira firm in the last two years; to date, the company hasn't received a single report of an adverse side-effect from customers or their doctors.

how to use it

St John's wort is best taken as a tablet with a standardized concentration of hypericin.

valerian
valeriana officinalis

what it is

Valerian is an attractive perennial with pretty pink flowers. It grows throughout Europe and is now well established in North America. As far back as the 1st century AD, the physician Dioscorides used it, as did Hippocrates before him, and Paracelsus after that.

In the Middle Ages, valerian was used for many medicinal purposes, though proof of its efficacy in the treatment of epilepsy has never been substantiated. While the ancient Greeks and Romans understood the herb's value as a gentle sedative, it wasn't until the middle of the 18th century that it became widely accepted in the treatment of anxiety and insomnia. Valerian contains many active constituents, including volatile oils, iridoids and alkaloids.

dosage

Up to 3 grams of dried plant, equivalent to 700mg of standardized extract. As tincture: 20 drops in a cup of hot water four times a day for anxiety, or half an hour before bed for insomnia.

precautions

There are no reported side-effects or interactions with prescribed medications. Valerian is safe to use during pregnancy or breast-feeding.

what it does

Prolonged periods of stress lead to a state of constant heightened arousal, and overproduction of the activity hormone **adrenaline**. This is the hormone that prepares the body for 'fight or flight' – the heart rate increases, blood pressure rises and mental faculties are sharpened so that mind and body are prepared for instant action.

Valerian can break this vicious cycle. Taken in small doses, its action is **calming** without causing drowsiness. Larger doses become mildly sedative and help to **restore** regular **sleep** patterns in those suffering from insomnia. As a bonus, valerian is an effective anti-spasmodic which helps to relieve **colic**, stomach cramps and **irritable bowel syndrome** (IBS).

how to use it

Most commonly taken as tablets, but see 'dosage' for alternatives.

vitality
boosters

What is vitality? Energy, vivacity, liveliness, strength, life, vigour, animation, verve, get-up-and-go, *joie de vivre* . . . in fact, it is a combination of them all. Vitality is being endowed with life and relishing everything it brings. Some people have it; sadly, most don't. Perhaps it is more accurate to say that we all have the vital life force known as *chi* to the Chinese, but not everyone is able to exploit it. Poor diet, stress, worry and tension sap away the vital force of life. The result? Many people go through the motions of living, but their lives are devoid of vitality.

How often do you see people slumped at their office desks, shambling along the street with heads bowed and shoulders drooped, wilting behind the supermarket checkout and avoiding the slightest risk of eye contact with the customers? How often have you gazed longingly at the one person who is the centre of attention at any party and wished it were you? Regardless of age, sex or physical appearance, some people's abundance of vitality is like a magnet, drawing others into their circle and lighting up the world around them. It has nothing to do with money, power, position or beauty; these people radiate a life force that is a combination of physical and emotional well-being.

The vitality boosters in this chapter are designed to help you make full use of your own life force. They range from the guarana seeds of the Brazilian rain forest with their life-giving energy, and the natural vitality boost of the phytoestrogens in red clover, to the remarkable BIO-STRATH elixir, a vitality tonic containing a complex mixture of many herbs. All these boosters are safe, powerful and effective, but of course, on their own the benefits are transitory. In emergencies, they can be a springboard, but they are not a crutch on which to limp through the rest of life. Combine them with good food, a good attitude and a lust for life, however, and you could discover a hidden depth of vitality you never knew you had.

bio-strath elixir

what it is

BIO-STRATH elixir is the only proprietary product listed in this book, and it is here for two reasons. Firstly, it is available in most parts of the world. Secondly, it is unique. BIO-STRATH is made by feeding a complex mixture of many medicinal herbs to a very special and nutritious variety of yeast. During the process, the yeast cells digest and absorb all the beneficial contents of the herbs. A fermentation process follows that ruptures the cell walls of the yeast, releasing the contents, which now include beneficial enzymes from the yeast. Organic honey and orange juice are added, resulting in an easily absorbed and amazingly versatile natural food supplement. For many years, this booster has been a favourite of some of the world's great elite athletes and leading show-business personalities: all people whose livelihoods and success depend on having that 'it' factor, which means unflagging vitality.

dosage

5 ml three times daily, doubled if necessary.

precautions

There are no reported adverse reactions or interactions with other medications. BIO-STRATH is suitable and, in fact, advisable to take throughout pregnancy and during breast-feeding. It is safe for children of all ages.

what it does

The Pestalozzi family who make BIO-STRATH on the edge of Lake Zurich in Switzerland have been involved in serious scientific research for more than 30 years. These studies have shown that the product has the effect of **boosting** natural **immunity**, increasing physical **endurance** and **performance**, enhancing **mental ability** and even helping to **protect** cancer patients against the side-effects of radiation treatment. In short, BIO-STRATH is vitality in a bottle. It is suitable for children, adults and the elderly, and because of its unique manufacturing process, it is very quickly absorbed into the body where it can start its work.

how to use it

This is one of the very few natural supplements that should be taken on a long-term and regular basis because it protects against infection and enhances performance. It is best taken before meals for optimum absorption.

evening primrose oil

what it is

Evening primrose oil is a rich source of gamma linolenic acid (GLA). This is what is known as a fatty acid and it has a valuable property of being converted by the body into a substance known as prostaglandin. Prostaglandins are one of the most powerful natural anti-inflammatories which also improve blood flow through the smallest of capillaries. Prostaglandins also have a role in helping to reduce the stickiness of blood, thus lessening the risk of clots and thrombosis.

The much more easily obtained linoleic acid is widespread in vegetable oils, seeds and nuts; in optimum circumstances this, too, may be converted into prostaglandins. Unfortunately, a variety of situations can interfere with the process, which is why gamma linolenic acid is such a sought-after and widely used natural booster. Borage oil and blackcurrant seed oil are also good sources of GLA, although the vast majority of research work has used evening primrose oil.

dosage

Up to 3 grams daily.

precautions

There are no reported adverse side-effects or interactions with prescribed medications. Evening primrose oil is safe and advisable during pregnancy and breast-feeding. It is suitable in smaller doses for children over the age of 12, particularly for the treatment of eczema.

what it does

Evening primrose oil is valuable in a wide range of inflammatory conditions such as **eczema**, **arthritis**, **tendonitis** and cyclic **breast lumps**. But from a vitality-boosting point of view, its greatest benefit is in the relief of **premenstrual syndrome**. There is nothing more draining of vitality than this wretched condition, which frequently deprives huge numbers of women of two weeks of their normal lives in every month. The **benefits** of GLA are much enhanced by the addition of vitamin B_6, zinc, magnesium and vitamin C, so it is always useful to combine capsules of evening primrose oil with these nutrients.

how to use it

For severe PMS, take 1 gram three times a day for the ten days before your next period is due. PMS in particular responds best if a concurrent daily supplement of vitamin B_6, zinc, magnesium and vitamin C is taken throughout the month.

what it is

Of all the medicinal plants of the Brazilian rain forest, the best known is guarana. Rain forest Indians have used this plant for many thousands of years as a tonic, stimulant and aid to vitality. Traditionally, the seeds are turned into hard sticks, which are then grated into boiling water to make guarana tea.

First discovered by the Maues-Sateres Indians, guarana was so valuable that they traded it as a form of money with neighbouring tribes. When the 17th-century missionary Bettendorf came across this group of Indians, he described them as the sturdiest and healthiest of all the tribes he found during his travels.

guarana
paulinia cupana

available as

Capsules
Chewing gum
Liquid extract

dosage

2 grams of guarana powder or grated stick in a cup of hot water will provide approximately 50mg of the active substance guaranine.

precautions

Although its caffeine content is very small, guarana should be avoided during pregnancy and breast-feeding. Do not take if you have high blood pressure or are caffeine-sensitive. Anyone with sleeping problems should avoid guarana late in the day.

what it does

Studies show that guarana increases **energy**, reduces **stress** and improves mood and **performance**. There are claims that the benefits of guarana are due to its caffeine content; the truth is that the prepared extracts act in a totally different way from caffeine and produce none of the side-effects of coffee, the world's most widely used stimulant drug. The amount of caffeine in a daily dose of guarana is, at 35mg, far less than that in a cola drink, less than half found in a cup of tea, and only about 15 per cent of the amount found in a cup of real coffee. The reason guarana works as a highly effective, **slow-release**, energy and vitality booster is that it is absorbed extremely slowly into the body. Because it is a member of the soapwood family, guarana is rich in natural fats, which account for this **beneficial** slow absorption.

Guarana is not an instant high, does not raise blood pressure, nor is it addictive. In fact, it has none of the side-effects of caffeine and is of enormous help in the treatment of ME, **chronic fatigue** and Tired All The Time Syndrome. On a day-to-day basis, it provides the vitality to cope with long hours of work, sporting endurance and even a night on the town.

how to use it

Guarana can be taken as capsules, liquid extracts, chewing gum or made into tea.

what it is

This perennial herb with its dark pink flowers is a native of Europe and Asia, but has become naturalised in Australia, New Zealand and the US. Agriculturally, red clover is an effective crop; like other clovers, its roots fix nitrogen into the soil, so it is often used as one of the regenerating plants in fallow fields. Traditionally used in both Chinese and European herbal medicine as an expectorant for bad coughs, for skin problems and as an external application for breast cancer, its most valuable properties were discovered by accident. A sheep farmer in New Zealand found that the fertility of his flock seemed to be in decline for no apparent reason. The sheep all looked healthy, they were well nourished and had not been fed on anything but what grew in the fields they grazed. The mystery was solved when they realized they were in a field full of red clover. Analysis revealed that the flowers of red clover are rich in the plant hormones called isoflavones, particularly genistein, which is known to have oestrogenic properties. The sheep were moved to another field without red clover and fertility returned to normal.

red clover
trifolium pratense

available as	dosage
capsules	2 to 3 grams of the dried
dried flowers	flowers in tablet form daily
tablets	three cups of tea, made with
tincture	dried flowers, and of tincture
	in warm water, three times daily

precautions

There are no reported side-effects or interactions with prescribed medications. Because of its oestrogenic properties, avoid during pregnancy or breast-feeding. Not suitable for children.

what it does

Because of its gentle **oestrogenic** effect, red clover certainly has some of the traditional properties that have been ascribed to it. As an **anti-inflammatory** in skin disease, as an **anti-cancer** agent and a heart-protector, this is a valuable plant. By far its most popular everyday use, however, is in the relief of **menopausal** symptoms.

Red clover is second to none as a vitality booster during difficult phases of the menopause, helping to control **mood swings**, hot flushes, depression and irritability. It also helps reduce the increased risk of **heart disease** in post-menopausal women.

how to use it

Take as a tea made from the dried flowers. For precise doses, extracts of red clover are available as tablets and capsules.

what it is

Growing to more than 6 metres (20ft) in length, this fragrant vine has pink flowers, red berries and an ancient history of use as a tonic in traditional Chinese medicine. The Chinese name *wu-wei-zi* translates as 'five-flavoured plant', and the berries do indeed have a very complex sweet, sour and salty flavour.

Schisandra is native to China and is widely cultivated for medicinal use. The plant is also found in nearby regions of Korea and Russia. As with many other traditional Chinese medicines, schisandra has become increasingly popular in the West, and is available from Chinese herbalists as well as traditional health-food stores.

schisandra
schisandra chinensis
wu-wei-zi

available as
Dried berries

dosage
Up to 5 grams a day of the fruit or 2ml of tincture three times a day.

precautions

There are no reported interactions with other medications, and virtually no adverse reactions. Rarely, some gastric disturbance or loss of appetite may occur. Avoid during pregnancy and breast-feeding.

what it does

Schisandra berries contain a complex mixture of natural substances including essential oils, **lignans** such as schizandrin and gomisin, phytosterols and a number of natural acids. Ancient Chinese texts maintain that schisandra is **invaluable** for the relief of **stress** and restoring the **zest** for life so essential for bounding vitality. Some modern research has also shown that this herb can be valuable in the treatment of **liver disease** and can help in the treatment of **hepatitis.**

Modern herbalists describe schisandra as an adaptogenic, which means it helps the body adapt to a whole range of stressful situations, thereby improving concentration and mental and physical strength. Folklore also ascribes powerful **aphrodisiac** effects to this extraordinary berry.

how to use it

The dried berries can be chewed or the active constituent can be obtained from using a tincture.

activity
boosters

Keeping active is one of the most important factors in maintaining good health, and the two essential requirements for activity are energy and mobility. An active lifestyle benefits the heart and circulatory system, improves breathing, maintains muscle strength, keeps joints mobile and releases the 'feel-good' endorphins from the brain that promote an overall sense of well-being.

Besides all of these points, an active lifestyle has other benefits. Weight-bearing exercise, for example, is a vital protector against osteoporosis, especially in women, and keeping on the go is the most effective way of weight control. Every hour spent as a couch potato burns up around 70 calories, so sitting for 20 minutes burns up just 25. Spend that 20 minutes walking one mile, however, and you'd burn 100. A five-mile walk consumes 500 calories; staying at home in front of the TV uses a mere 130.

The activity supplements listed in this chapter are a mixture of energy boosters and joint protectors. Some are also anti-inflammatory – which means that if you're already suffering from joint damage, they will reduce pain, enabling you to be more active. After all, more activity means greater muscle strength, and better muscles mean less pain – and, of course, better health.

available as
Fresh chillies
Capsules
Dried powder (for cooking)
Prescription-only cream

chilli
capsicum frutescens

what it is

The chilli is one of the many culinary and medicinal plants brought back to Europe from the Americas by the Spaniards during the 16th century. Its original home is believed to be Mexico, where it has always been valued as both food and medicine, and where it still plays a major role in the traditions of Mexican cookery.

The chilli is a member of the *solanaceae* family, which includes potatoes, tomatoes, sweet peppers, aubergines and deadly nightshade. It has many close relations varying in intensity and flavour from the sweet (bell) pepper and mild Hungarian paprika to the extremely hot varieties like Birdseye, common in Thai cuisine, which should only be handled with gloves.

dosage

500mg dried powder once or twice daily in capsule form.

precautions

Chilli as used in normal food recipes is safe, but avoid it in higher doses for medicinal purposes during pregnancy or breast-feeding. Avoid internal use of therapeutic doses if you have ulcers or ulcerative colitis. Do not use for medicinal purposes in babies and children under two.

what it does

All chillies contain the natural chemical capsaicin, which is responsible for the fruit's traditional use as a circulatory **stimulant**. Its warming action increases blood flow to painful joints, helping to relieve **arthritic** and rheumatic pain. This effect can be enhanced by applying it in cream form locally over damaged **joints**; the increased blood flow is immediately apparent as the skin reddens. Taken internally, chilli is a good **digestive** and also an effective natural **anti-bacterial** – which, of course, makes it a strong activity booster.

how to use it

Use either as dried powder, or as whole or deseeded chillis (often chopped) in food. Chillis can also be taken as a tincture: 5ml of powder dissolved in 25ml of water. Massage with chilli oil – put four small hot chillis into 500ml of olive or grape seed oil; keeps for a month in cool place. Excellent for arthritic joints and aching muscles.

coenzyme Q$_{10}$

what it is

Coenzyme Q$_{10}$ is a powerful antioxidant present in virtually every cell of the body. It occurs naturally in beef, peanuts, spinach, broccoli and oily fish such as sardines, though most of it is manufactured in the body from other forms of coenzyme Q.

Even though it is available from foodstuffs, coenzyme Q$_{10}$ is a valuable supplement that helps recovery from some of the more distressing conditions that are so rife in modern society. Glandular fever, chronic fatigue syndrome, Tired All The Time syndrome and ME are all conditions that benefit from its natural and gentle energy boost. It is also helpful alongside St John's wort for the treatment of depression, as fatigue, exhaustion and constant need to sleep are frequently all symptoms of this sad condition.

dosage

30 to 90mg per day.

precautions

There are no reported side-effects from this supplement, but no studies have been done to establish its safety during pregnancy and breast-feeding.

what it does

The powerful **antioxidant** properties of coenzyme Q_{10} make it a potent protector against free-radical damage at the cellular level. Adequate amounts are essential for **protection** against **heart disease** and **cancer**, but it has another function much more appropriate to activity levels.

Coenzyme Q_{10} is the vital link that completes the complex chemical processes through which the body converts food into available energy. Research indicates that the body's ability to manufacture this vital substance declines with age, and levels may be considerably reduced in older people. Though this supplement may be helpful in a variety of specific conditions, its main **benefit** is to provide an increase of available **energy**. Reduced levels of coenzyme Q_{10} mean that calories from food cannot be efficiently converted into energy that the body can utilize.

how to use it

30mg once daily should be the starting dose. This may be increased to one 30mg capsule three times a day if required. Coenzyme Q_{10} is better absorbed in the presence of oils, so a teaspoon of olive oil or peanut butter taken with the capsule improves absorption.

what it is

This extraordinary plant is the traditional anti-inflammatory medicine of the bushmen who roam the Kalahari Sands of Namibia. They hunt under the blazing desert sun for their favourite medicine, digging huge holes to expose the large tubers and roots produced by this tiny flowering plant.

Devil's claw gets its name from its viciously barbed seed pod, which resembles two sets of claws back to back. The pod hooks itself into the hairy feet of animals that roam the Kalahari, thus ensuring its distribution throughout the desert. The pod survives until the next rains, when it germinates and sends its roots deep into the desert sands. For the bushmen, this plant is a lifesaver as well as an anti-inflammatory: they drink its bitter juice when no water can be found.

devil's claw
harpagophytum procumbens

available as
Capsules
Liquid extracts
Tablets

dosage
500mg standardized extract twice daily, equivalent to 2.2 grams per capsule of whole devil's claw root.

precautions

Diabetics should take devil's claw only under medical supervision, as it may reduce the need for insulin. Those with duodenal or gastric ulcers should avoid devil's claw, because its iridoid glycosides improve digestion by increasing the production of stomach acid.

what it does

Devil's claw contains the natural glycosides known as harpagoside, harpagide and procumbide. It is probable that these powerful substances are responsible for the tubers' **anti-inflammatory** effects.

A double-blind trial of devil's claw tablets produced significant reductions in **shoulder**, **neck** and **back** pain from as early as two weeks into the study. Another study conducted in Parisian hospitals showed impressive results in the relief of arthritic pain. If your activity is impaired by gout, arthritis, **rheumatism** or muscle pain, then devil's claw could bring safe and effective **relief**.

how to use it

Take devil's claw tablets twice daily (morning and evening) with food.

what it is

Glucosamine sulphate is a natural chemical derived from sugars. Very little of it comes from food, and it is largely manufactured by the body. It is essential for the manufacture of one of the many mucopolysaccharides – specifically glycosaminoglycan, which is an essential component of cartilage. There is evidence that the body produces less glucosamine sulphate with age.

Many athletes now use glucosamine in supplement form to overcome damage to cartilage structure of weight-bearing joints. This is particularly important for gymnasts, ballet dancers and long-distance runners. Extra glucosamine also offers a degree of protection against degenerative damage, as well as pain reduction, which improves mobility.

glucosamine sulphate

available as
Tablets

dosage
500mg three times daily.

precautions

There are no reports of toxicity, or of adverse interaction with any other medications.

what it does

Glucosamine sulphate has two main functions: promoting **regrowth** of damaged **cartilage** and reducing inflammation and pain in arthritic joints. The protective layer of cartilage covering the bony surfaces of joints is damaged and destroyed by **osteoarthritis**. Loss of this cartilage results in roughening of the bony surfaces, **pain** and **swelling** in affected joints and immobility.

Glucosamine has been used in Europe since the early 1980s, and many clinical studies have demonstrated its ability to relieve pain and swelling, and also to reverse some of the damage done to the cartilage in arthritic joints. Previously dry, thin and brittle cartilaginous tissue becomes thicker, smoother and more **pliable** after just one month of taking the supplement.

A trend in recent years has combined glucosamine sulphate with chondroitin – extracted from shark's cartilage – but there is no clinical evidence that chondroitin improves the efficacy of this wonderful supplement. All major trials done with glucosamine alone show how effective it is at improving activity levels by restoring better function to damaged joints.

how to use it

Should be taken by anyone suffering from arthritic joint disease. The recommended intake is 1,500 mg per day in three equal doses, usually taken as tablets.

kelp
laminaria (various species)

what it is

Many seaweeds are often described as kelp, but the term applies to some members
of both the *Laminaria* and *Fucus* family. Most varieties occur only in the northern seas,
and have been used traditionally in agriculture and medicine for hundreds of years.
From Cornwall to the west coast of Ireland, from the Channel Islands to the Hebrides,
kelp has been prepared by drying, burning and reconstituting.

Other varieties of seaweed, especially in China and Japan, have long been highly
regarded as food and medicine. With modern knowledge of the nutritional value of
seaweeds, I find it extraordinary that the whole world isn't rushing to put them on
its shopping list.

dosage

One tablet daily of dried kelp, providing no more than 250 micrograms of iodine.

precautions

Fresh seaweed can contain large amounts of salt, so anyone with high blood pressure should avoid it. Due to the iodine content, do not take or use in cooking if you're pregnant or breast-feeding. Seek advice from your doctor before using any form of kelp if you have a thyroid problem.

what it does

Folklore tells us that dried seaweed lowers **blood pressure**, cures stomach **ulcers**, prevents goitre and protects against some forms of cancer. In nutritional terms, these ancient remedies certainly work. Although there are slight variations in the make-up of different varieties, the importance of adding seaweed to the diet cannot be overstated. Most are an excellent source of protein, but low in calories. They are also full of soluble fibre, extremely rich in calcium and magnesium, a tremendous source of **beta-carotene**, rich in potassium, exceptionally well supplied with **iron** and **zinc** and by far the richest source of natural iodine of all foods. For vegetarians and vegans, seaweeds are a real must because of their vitamin B_{12} content. From an activity standpoint, the major importance of kelp is its **iodine** content – an essential mineral lacking in many people's diets. Iodine is vital for the normal function of the **thyroid** gland, which in turn controls many bodily functions. Taking extra kelp can make you feel more active and aid in **weight loss**, which is important if obesity is contributing to your lack of activity. The iron content also protects against anaemia, another common cause of lethargy.

how to use it

Kelp tablets should be taken once daily at a maximum dose of 250 micrograms of iodine. Kelp can also be used in cooking as fresh seaweed, or as dried kelp powder added to soups, stews and sauces.

ginseng
panax (various species)

what it is

Panax ginseng, also known as Chinese or Korean ginseng, has been used as a medicine for more than 6,000 years. Such was its value that the ancient warlords battled for the ground where it grew. It is related to the American ginseng, *Panax quinquefolius,* and less closely to Siberian ginseng, *Eleutherococcus senticosus*. Ginseng is grown for its root, which is harvested in the autumn and preserved by drying. *Panax ginseng* contains many active chemicals, the most important of which are ginsenosides – researchers have already identified more than 20 different ginsenosides in every root.

dosage

Up to 1.5 grams a day of dried root or extract.

precautions

Ginseng should not be taken by anyone with high blood pressure, or during pregnancy or breast-feeding. Keep coffee consumption to a minimum while taking ginseng, as the two together may cause hyper-excitability.

what it does

Although introduced to Europe around 800 AD, it wasn't until the 1700s that a real understanding of ginseng's amazing energy- and activity-boosting properties were discovered. Though folklore offers a rich vein of stories about ginseng's **virility-enhancing** effects, the real value of this strange root is as an aid to physical activity and energy. In China, it was especially recommended to boost activity and mental **prowess** in the elderly.

There is now good evidence that this supplement **strengthens** the body's natural **immune system**, thus increasing resistance to **infection**. It also helps the fight against **stress**, so it is a great short-term aid during excessively difficult periods: bereavement, divorce, redundancy, moving house, exams, etc.

how to use it

For short-term use only: two or three weeks, then at least a two-week break. In extreme circumstances, take for six weeks followed by four without. Do not use ginseng in the evening as it may cause over-stimulation and insomnia. Best taken as capsules containing dried root and extract, or as a liquid tonic which supplies a daily equivalent of 1,250 mg.

pycnogenols

what it is

The bark of many trees has been used as a source of medicine for thousands of years. Willow bark was a treatment for pain relief, Cinchona bark is used as an anti-malarial in the rain forests, Pacific yew is now a cancer treatment – but its benefits were discovered long ago by the North American Indians. Products based on these trees have a long and respected use in conventional medicine, but substances yielded by the bark of the Mediterranean pine, though taken for generations by local people, have only recently found their way into wider use.

Mediterranean pine bark produces a group of powerful antioxidants called pycnogenols, or OPCs (oligomeric proanthocyanidins). These valuable flavonoids are widely distributed in foods, but the Mediterranean pine is the richest source.

dosage

50 to 100 mg per day.

precautions

There are no reported toxic side-effects or interactions with other medications.

what it does

Pycnogenols have two major functions: they are powerful antioxidants which protect against **free-radical** damage, especially to the heart and circulatory system; and they are crucial to the integrity of collagen and elastin, a vital part of joint, **muscle** and cartilage structure. Pycnogenols provide a huge boost to the amount of activity possible for those suffering a wide range of joint problems, especially soft-tissue conditions like tennis or golfer's **elbow**, frozen **shoulder** and **cartilage** damage.

One of the most interesting recent studies examined the performance of a group of healthy athletic students at California State University in America. The volunteers were divided into two groups: one given pycnogenols, the other a placebo. The object of the experiment was to measure the exercise endurance of the athletes. Amazingly, those taking the supplement showed a 21 per cent increase in overall endurance as **super-antioxidants**, pycnogenols, protected against damaging free radicals released during exercise. For this reason, anyone following an intense training and exercise programme could benefit from increasing their antioxidant intake.

how to use it

Most commonly taken as a capsule or tablet containing 30 to 50 mg. Up to 100 mg per day is a normal dose.

aphrodisiac
boosters

Named after Aphrodite, the goddess of love, aphrodisiacs are foods or medicines that help to engender feelings of romance, trigger emotional arousal, increase libido and enhance sexual performance and enjoyment. Historically, aphrodisiacs are as ancient as mankind. Although used widely on every continent and in every age, mainstream medical opinion has always maintained that their effects are more psychological than physiological.

That is, of course, until the arrival of Viagra™ and the flood of research and interest this drug has generated. While psychological factors can be detrimental to relationships and lovemaking, many straightforward physical problems can be helped by the natural remedies included in this chapter. Zinc, for example, is essential for the formation of sperm and male sexuality, yet is commonly deficient in the Western diet. One of the richest natural sources is the oyster, so it is hardly surprising that Casanova is reputed to have eaten 70 a day – usually while sharing a bath with his latest conquest.

As sperm counts decline rapidly and infertility problems increase year by year, many people are turning to traditional plants and nutritional remedies as a solution to their problems – and as the facts testify, they often work. In my own practice, I've seen many patients save relationships, improve their sex lives and raise wonderful families by using natural medicines to improve circulation, reduce the size of enlarged prostates and rekindle the flames of passion.

All the remedies listed here are safe to use, have no side-effects and are easily available at your health-food store or pharmacy. So, if your love life is lacklustre, or your passion for a family is unfulfilled, why not give them a try before resorting to much more complex and invasive medical treatments?

catuaba
anemopaegma arvense

what it is

A Brazilian proverb states that 'Until a father reaches 60, the son is his; after that the son is catuaba's.' There are two species of catuaba. The first is a tree found in the northern regions of Brazil, which grows to an immense height; the second is found in the central areas of Espírito Santo and Minas Gerais and takes the form of a large, bushy shrub. Both types are equally effective medicinally, and a traditional herbal tea is prepared from the bark of each. As catuaba tea has a very bitter flavour, the Brazilians sweeten it with a little honey. Never ones to do things by halves, they may also mix the tea with their own lethal cane-sugar brandy, cachaça.

dosage

Up to 1 gram of
dried bark daily.

precautions

There are no reported
side-effects.

what it does

This most famous of all the Brazilian aphrodisiac plants has been used
by the indigenous population for generations. In spite of the extensive
use and enormous popularity of catuaba, little research has been
conducted into its chemical structure or active ingredients, although
it does include **tannins**, aromatic **oils** and **phytosterols** (natural
plant steroid alcohols).

Brazilian herbalists describe catuaba as a central nervous system
stimulant with aphrodisiac properties, and it is prescribed for
impotence, debility, agitation and sexual **weakness**. While the
aphrodisiac effects are most dramatic in men for the treatment
of impotence, catuaba is also regarded as **beneficial** for women.
When the World Health Organization surveyed more than 100 Brazilian
plants with reputed aphrodisiac properties, catuaba was one of only
three considered worthy of further investigation.

how to use it

One to three cups a day
of tea made from the
bark. Tea can also be
made by emptying one
capsule into a cup and
adding boiling water.

muira puama
ptychopetalum
(various types)

what it is

Muira puama is another native bushy tree from the Brazilian rain forest and is especially prolific in the Amazonas and Rio Negro regions. The different species vary in height from 5 to 15 metres (16½ to 46ft), with a greyish trunk, white flowers and green fruit which gradually change to pink, then to purple-black when ripe. Although in rain forest Indian medicine various parts of the plant have been used, in modern times the woody bark and roots are the sources of herbal extracts. The plant is rich in sterols, esters and volatile oil containing humulene, pinenes, camphene, beta-caryophyllene and the specific alkaloid muirapuamine.

dosage

1.5 grams daily of
alcoholic extract

precautions

There are no reported
side-effects or risks.

what it does

The common name of this plant in Brazil is '**potency** wood' and
it is for the treatment of male impotence and the improvement of
sexual function that this remedy is best known. Its use for this
purpose is part of Amazon tribal folklore, but it also has a long history
as a **nerve tonic** and a treatment for diarrhoea.

Brought to the UK by the early explorers, muira puama has been
a traditional **medicine** among British herbalists for many years, and
is listed in the *British Herbal Pharmacopoeia*. Unlike most traditional
aphrodisiacs, it has been the subject of a number of clinical trials in
which **beneficial** effects on erectile problems were seen in between
51 and 62 per cent of patients taking 1.5 grams of extract every day.

how to use it

Capsules are available
and usually combine
muira puama with other
stimulants such as ginseng.
Active ingredients are not
water soluble so infusions,
capsules and tablets are
not recommended. Use as
a hot, extracted alcoholic
tincture: one part herb to
five parts alcohol, at a
dose of 1.5 grams of
tincture daily.

what it is

Pfaffia is another native of the Amazon basin, but it is also common throughout Peru, Venezuela and Ecuador. This shrub-like vine forms a large, rambling plant, which houses most of its therapeutic properties within a complex root system. It was first described by the great South American botanist Carl von Martius in the mid-1800s and later named *Pfaffia paniculata*. By the beginning of the 20th century, it seemed to have disappeared from Western herbal literature.

Until 1975, that is. In that year, the Brazilian herbalist, Jeff, met a shaman of the Xingu tribe who extolled the virtues of pfaffia, the secrets of which had been passed from shaman to shaman in this tribe for 1,000 years. As an aphrodisiac, for wound healing, in the treatment of diabetes and even for the relief of cancer, pfaffia appears to be a cure-all, or panacea. This is why it is universally known as Brazilian ginseng – the Latin name for ginseng is *panax* from the Greek *panacea*. Throughout Brazil, this amazing plant is known as *para todo* – "for everything", in Portuguese.

pfaffia
Pfaffia paniculata
brazilian ginseng

available as
Capsules

dosage
1 to 4 grams of dried powder, in divided doses of 500mg

precautions

No side-effects have been reported,
but because of its plant hormone
content, avoid during pregnancy
and breast-feeding.

what it does

Pfaffia has a proven ability to combat **stress** and work as an
effective aphrodisiac. A number of Japanese scientists isolated
three chemicals from the plant – pfaffocides D, E and F – which
inhibit the growth of cultured cancerous **tumour** cells.

The plant also contains significant amounts of the mineral
germanium, with beta-carotene, B vitamins, other minerals
and essential amino acids, as well as three extraordinary plant
hormones: beta-ecdysone, sitosterol and stigmasterol. These
three probably account for pfaffia's value in the treatment
of **PMS** and **menopausal** symptoms, and make it a safe
alternative for women not able to use conventional HRT.

The combination of stimulant and plant hormones makes pfaffia
an ideal aphrodisiac which helps both men and women enjoy
sexual fulfilment. This remarkable herb is also useful in the
treatment of glandular fever, **ME**, chronic fatigue and Tired All The
Time Syndrome. Many athletes find that it helps to build **muscle
strength** and endurance thanks to the plant hormones, but has
none of the dangerous side-effects of the illegal anabolic steroids.

how to use it

Take as capsules of the
dried root. Use up to
a maximum of eight
capsules daily, at times
of severe stess. Do not
take late in the evening as
it might keep you awake.

what it is

What did Casanova know that you don't? To the poet, music may be the 'food of love', but in reality it's oysters. Casanova, the greatest lover of all time, used to eat 70 a day which he claimed as the reason for his super-stud performance.

Oysters have been a favourite aphrodisiac food for centuries, dating back to Roman times. What they didn't know as they ate vast quantities of native Colchester oysters – the best in the world – was that these bivalves contained substantial quantities of zinc, a mineral that is essential for the production of sperm and the maintenance of male potency. A dozen of these magnificent molluscs provide more than you need for a whole week.

zinc & oyster extract

available as

Capsules

dosage

100mg pure oyster extract, plus 15mg of zinc in a single daily dose.

Apart from allergic reactions by
those who are sensitive to oysters,
there are no known side-effects.

what it does

For those who don't like the flavour or texture of oysters, taking them
as an extract is the perfect alternative – so long as you are not allergic
to shellfish. Oysters are a good source of **protein** and an excellent
source of vitamin B_{12}, **zinc** and copper. They provide useful amounts
of vitamin E, iron, potassium, thiamine, riboflavin, selenium and **folic
acid**. The combination of all these **nutrients** plus the additional
15mg of zinc not only has a specific and beneficial effect on libido and
performance, but also enhances general **health**, is heart-protective,
cancer-fighting and a powerful **mood** booster.

how to use it

Take as a one-a-day
capsule of pure oyster
extract plus zinc.

cleansing
boosters

Just as your house benefits from spring cleaning, your body needs the occasional spring clean, too. Ideally, this should take the form of a quarterly detox programme conducted in association with the three-day detox diet shown on pages 138–9. The regime works wonders at the end of a long winter, as a preparation for summer holidays or the onslaughts of cold weather and to cleanse your system after the excesses of Christmas.

Our bodies are faced with a vast range of toxic pollutants in the air we breathe and the food we eat. Central heating and air conditioning leave most workplaces drier than the Sahara Desert, and the proliferation of electronic gadgetry fills the atmosphere with ozone and irritating carbon particles. Our food is not only full of additives, preservatives, flavourings, colourings and unwanted E numbers, but it also overflows with salt and fats. Salt encourages fluid retention, bloating and discomfort, while added fats put additional stresses on the liver and digestive system.

Using the detox plan a few times a year will help in the war against pollutants and additives, but super-cleansing boosters can assist your body at any time. Extracts of artichoke stimulate the gall bladder and liver, improve fat digestion and prove a useful antidote to excessive alcohol. Dandelion leaves eliminate excess fluid. Milk thistle helps to cleanse the liver, while dong quai purifies the blood and makes a particularly useful cleansing tonic for women.

artichoke
cynara scolymus
globe

what it is

Every French housewife knows that the globe artichoke is a boon to the digestion and a powerful stimulant of the gall bladder and liver. Globe artichokes are a type of thistle that originates from the Mediterranean part of Europe. These are not to be confused with the Jerusalem artichoke, a North American plant which found its way to France during the 1600s. The latter, a knobbly little tuber related to the sunflower, is rich in potassium but not much else.

dosage

300 to 600mg of standardized extract or 10 to 20 grams fresh leaf daily.

precautions

There are no reported side-effects or interactions with other medications.

what it does

Rich in a bitter chemical called cynarine, artichokes traditionally form the first course of any over-rich meal. Because they **stimulate** the production of bile, this makes the **digestion** of fats much easier. Bile works in the same way as washing-up liquid on greasy dishes: it breaks fat down into minute globules, dramatically increasing the surface area that is exposed to the stomach's digestive juices.

Herbalists have traditionally used extracts of artichoke to treat **high blood pressure**, and it is also known to help the body get rid of **cholesterol**. Together with its diuretic properties, artichoke is a **cleanser** and **detoxifier** – which makes it useful for people suffering from gout, arthritis or rheumatism.

Both types of artichoke also contain a plant chemical called inulin; like **fibre**, inulin is not broken down during digestion, but is fermented in the colon (large bowel). It has a similar action to fibre, but can be an embarrassing source of flatulence.

how to use it

Eat fresh baby globe artichokes raw with a little olive oil, or sauté lightly and mix with pasta. You can also cook the leaves together with the peeled, chopped stalks for additional cynarine.

Standardized extracts are available as capsules and can be taken as a liver protector before and after rich food or a night on the town. Jerusalem artichokes are best eaten as soup.

available as

Capsules
Dried root
Fresh plant
Liquid extract
Tablets

dandelion
taraxacum officinale

what it is

It is no surprise that the French call this plant *pis en lit* and that the English country name for it is 'wet the bed'. *Pis en lit* salad is available in street markets throughout France.

The dandelion is a common plant that grows throughout the world. Related to chicory, its leaves have a similarly bitter taste. The name comes from the French *dent-de-lion* – a reference to the shape of the leaves, which some say resemble lion's teeth. For all gardeners seeking a perfect lawn, dandelions are a bane, but the leaves are delicious in salads and, apart from their medicinal value, are a rich source of iron. They are also valuable for their roots, which, when dried and ground, can be used as a coffee substitute.

dosage

3 to 5 grams of dried root, 5ml of alcoholic tincture or 200mg standardized extract may all be taken up to three times a day.

precautions

Avoid dandelion preparations while pregnant or breast-feeding. Do not use for severe fluid retention before consulting your doctor, and do not take in large doses if you have gallstones.

what it does

Dandelions contain carotenoids (including lutein), potassium, vitamin C, taraxacoside, taraxerol and **iron**. This cleansing herb is a strong **diuretic**, **tonic** and **anti-inflammatory**; there is even some evidence of anti-tumour benefits. Useful for **kidney** and **liver** problems, it also reduces fluid retention – especially around period time. Thanks to its eliminative properties, dandelions are also helpful for those with **rheumatism**.

how to use it

As long as dogs and cats are kept away from your lawn, you, too, can enjoy the unique flavour and all the health-giving benefits of young, bright-green dandelion leaves added to a salad. Eat the leaves raw or use a prepared alcoholic extract or dried-root herbal extract. Commercial products are available as liquid or tablets.

what it is

Dong quai, or Chinese angelica, is a most attractive plant, growing to about 1.8 metres (6 ft) tall with hollow stems, bright-green leaves and boasting abundant clusters of white flowers between May and August. A close relative of celery, it has been used in traditional Chinese medicine for more than 5,000 years. Ancient Chinese physicians called this plant 'female ginseng', and it is prescribed to this day for the treatment of menstrual and menopausal problems.

The ancient Chinese physicians regarded dong quai as second in importance only to ginseng for its powerful tonic actions. It has taken the Western world several millennia to catch up with Eastern medicine, and dong quai is one of the newer additions to the general herbal repertoire.

dong quai
chinese angelica

available as
Capsules
Dried powdered root

dosage
Up to 3 grams per day
of dried powdered root.

precautions

There are no reported interactions with other medications. Excessive dosage may cause sensitivity to sunlight in fair-skinned people. Not recommended during pregnancy or breast-feeding.

what it does

Dong quai is remarkable for its ability to help women with **menstrual** and menopausal problems. It is a powerful **tonic**, useful in the treatment of **iron** deficiency, **fatigue** and **pallor**, particularly when associated with heavy menstrual blood loss. It also has a strong anti-spasmodic action, and is effective in the relief of menstrual **cramps** and painful periods.

Where blood loss is scanty during the period, dong quai helps stimulate blood flow and acts as a uterine **cleanser** by helping eliminate collected debris. For this reason, it is better not to use dong quai immediately before or during menstruation if blood loss is normally heavy, though it is safe during the rest of the cycle. One of the key constituents is the volatile oil ligustilide, but the plant is also rich in coumarins and vitamin B_{12}.

how to use it

As capsules of standardized extract and powdered root. Use one teaspoon of powdered root to a cup of boiling water (have two a day), or half a teaspoon of tincture in a glass of water three times daily.

flax

linum usitatissimum

what it is

Flax is one of the most ancient of all cultivated plants, and is known to have been used by man since 5,000 BC. Egyptian mummies were wrapped in cloth made from the stems of flax, and this extraordinary plant is mentioned in the ancient writings of Greece, Rome and Egypt, as well as in the Old Testament. Both the seeds and seed oil have medicinal value.

Linoleic and linolenic essential fatty acids are both present in the oil, both essential precursors to the anti-inflamatory prostaglandins. Just like evening primrose oil this is what makes flax seed (linseed) oil such a valuable remedy for inflammatory skin and joint disorders.

dosage

One teaspoon of seeds or 1 to 3 grams of oil daily.

precautions

Taking excessive amounts of seeds and too little water may cause bowel obstruction. Take seeds separately from other medications, as they may slow drug absorption.

what it does

Flax seeds are an excellent laxative and have a cleansing effect on the entire **digestive** system. They are also useful for the reduction of **inflammation** of the stomach as well as of the small and large intestines. They can be an effective remedy for irritable bowel syndrome (IBS) and **diverticulitis**, and help to repair damage done by laxative abuse.

The oil is a rich source of **essential fatty acids** and can be used for the treatment of inflammatory joint problems, **eczema** and psoriasis. Crushed flax seeds make an effective poultice for the cleansing of boils and other skin infections.

Flax seeds are a useful aid to **cholesterol** reduction. Some studies have shown them to have cancer-fighting properties as well.

how to use it

As a laxative, soak one teaspoon of seeds in cold water overnight; eat them in the morning. For inflammatory problems, use crushed (but not powdered) seeds and take one teaspoon with a large glass of water daily for maximum oil release. For severe inflammatory problems, use capsules of oil, usually 1,250 mg per capsule, taken one to three times daily.

milk thistle
silybum marianum

what it is

Milk thistle belongs to the same family as the artichoke. It grows wild on roadside verges, derelict sites and in most gardens. The plant's vivid purple flower heads are a favourite with flower arrangers, but the seeds of the dried flowers are used medicinally.

The plant has been employed as a medicine since the birth of Christ, and the great English herbalist, Nicholas Culpeper, recommended it as a treatment for liver disorders during the 1700s. The seeds contain a complicated bioflavonoid called silymarin, and it is this that has the liver-protective and -stimulating activity.

dosage

15 grams of ground seeds made
into tea or 420 mg of standardized
silymarin are normal daily doses.

precautions

There are no reported side-effects,
and this herb is safe to use during
pregnancy and breast-feeding.
There are no reports of interactions
with other medications.

what it does

In traditional herbal medicine, milk thistle was used to kick-start
and increase the flow of milk for nursing mothers. Like many other
bitter herbs it also has a long history of use as a digestive and
appetite stimulant.

Milk thistle's silymarin content protects the **liver** from poisonous
toxins, and has even been used against poisoning by the death
cap mushroom. Its other important action is to stimulate the
regrowth of liver cells to replace those damaged by **disease** or
toxic substances. Like the artichoke, milk thistle **stimulates** the gall
bladder and helps the digestion of fatty foods, as well as **cleansing**
the liver after excessive consumption of alcohol or rich dishes.

how to use it

**Take up to 420 mg of
standardized silymarin
per day as capsules.
Use 5 grams of ground
seeds to a cup of boiling
water and drink up to
three cups of tea daily.**

digestive
boosters

In health terms, the digestive system is the body's poor relation. It doesn't have the drama attached to the heart, the mystery of the brain, or the urgency of the lungs. And until something goes wrong, we take it very much for granted.
The truth is that the whole system, from the time food goes in at one end until the residue comes out of the other, is the vital key to our very existence. If the digestive process is not working efficiently, then the body is unable to extract nutrients from food and transport them to every cell in the body enabling growth, activity, repair and replacement. In short: no digestion, no life.

The healthy gut contains around 2 kilograms (4½ lb) of 'good bugs' – probiotic bacteria – and produces approximately 4 litres (7 pints) of gas a day. Digestion starts with the enzymes in saliva, followed by hydrochloric acid and digestive juices in the stomach, and nutrient extraction in the small and large bowel. Poor food, rushed meals, too much fat, salt and sugar, too little fibre and probiotics can wreak havoc with the entire system. In addition, alcohol, caffeine, nicotine and many over-the-counter drugs can cause physical damage to the intestinal tract.

Nature provides us with a range of digestive boosters that stimulate and improve digestion as well as protecting these vital tissues. The bacteria in live yoghurt, the antacid properties of mint, the stimulating and anti-nausea function of ginger and the soothing effects of chamomile are just a small part of this story. Using these superboosters will not only help overcome many problems of the digestive system, it will also improve its efficiency and offer protection. Despite the benefits of these boosters, however, you cannot live on a junk-food diet, abuse your stomach and bowels and get away unscathed. An occasional binge is one thing, but constant abuse will result in serious consequences, from ulcers to diverticulitis, irritable bowel syndrome or even cancer of the bowel.

available as

Capsules

Dried herb

Fresh herb

Tablets

Tea bags

Tincture

chamomile

chamomilla recutita
german chamomile

what it is

German chamomile grows throughout Europe, often wild, but it is cultivated on a large scale for medicinal use. It has been a valuable herb since Roman times and was extremely popular with medieval herbalists. In southern Europe, chamomile tea is used extensively as a gentle, safe remedy for children. This attractive member of the daisy family has a deliciously sweet aroma and was often planted for lawns so that its fragrance was released when walked on. Used externally as lotions and creams, chamomile makes a soothing application for skin irritation, abrasions, bites and stings, but it is as a digestive aid that it has earned its reputation.

dosage

One teaspoon of tincture in a glass of water after each meal. If taking tablets or capsules, use the equivalent of 2 grams of plant per day. For tea, see 'how to use it'.

precautions

Chamomile has no known interactions with other medications, and is safe to use during pregnancy and breast-feeding. There have been rare reports of allergic reactions, more likely in people allergic to ragweed and chrysanthemums.

what it does

Chamomile flowers contain **volatile oils**, the most important of which are proazulenes, alpha-bisabolol and spiroether, together with bioflavonoids and quercetin. This combination is **anti-inflammatory** and **anti-spasmodic**, which accounts for its 2,000 year history in the treatment of digestive problems. This herb is particularly beneficial in the **relief** of irritable bowel syndrome, stomach cramp, bloating and colic. Weak chamomile tea with a little honey is excellent for children with a temperature, **headache** and **restlessness**.

how to use it

Chamomile is most simply taken as a tea: one teaspoon of dried flowers to a cup of boiling water. If using a tincture: one teaspoon to a glass of water.

fennel
foeniculum vulgare

what it is

Originally found growing wild throughout Europe, fennel is now widely cultivated around the world and has a history dating back to the ancient Greeks and Romans. Prime among its many medicinal uses are its beneficial effects on the digestive system, but the ancients also used it as an aid to slimming, due to its function as a strong appetite suppressant. Both the seeds and the delicate fronds are used widely in cooking, particularly in stews, soups and with fish dishes. The crushed seeds, together with dill, are a basic ingredient of babies' gripe water.

dosage

Half a teaspoon of crushed seeds to a cup of boiling water: drink three cups a day. Tincture: half a teaspoon in water three times a day.

precautions

There are no reports of interactions with other medications, but fennel seeds are toxic if taken in large amounts. They can badly affect the nervous system and cause convulsions, so do not exceed the recommended dose. Though there are no reports of fennel causing problems during pregnancy, it is probably best avoided.

what it does

The most important natural chemicals in fennel are anethole and fenchone, now thought to have **oestrogen**-like properties and also to have a specific effect on smooth muscle **contraction**. For this reason, fennel is invaluable in the treatment of constipation, irritable bowel syndrome (IBS), **colic** and **indigestion**. Seeds also stimulate the production of bile, thus improving **liver function** and fat digestion. In India and the Middle East, it is common to chew a few fennel seeds after a meal to improve digestion and prevent flatulence.

how to use it

Fennel seeds may be chewed or used to make tea. The plant can also be made into a tincture. And, of course, eat it as a vegetable.

what it is

This strongly aromatic spice is native to the eastern Mediterranean and North Africa. It grows wild on any odd pieces of waste ground, but is widely cultivated for its culinary and medicinal purposes. The ancient Egyptians used it as one of the ingredients of embalming fluid, and there are prescriptions that include fenugreek in the historical *Ebers papyrus*, which was compiled 3,500 years ago. Medicinally, the seeds are used, and due to their bitter taste, they are usually available 'debittered'. In India, *methi* – the dried leaves – are added to root-vegetable dishes for their strong taste and smell.

fenugreek
trigonella foenum-graecum

available as
Seeds

dosage
25 to 75 grams of seeds per day.

precautions

There are no reports of interactions with other medications, and fenugreek is extremely safe to use in cooking. However, the seeds should not be eaten during pregnancy as they may produce contractions of the uterus. Do not exceed 100 grams of seeds per day.

what it does

Fenugreek is a great remedy for constipation, and for the reduction of blood **cholesterol**. The seeds contain plant steroids, particularly saponins and flavonoids, and vitamins A and C, along with small amounts of minerals. They were traditionally prescribed during **convalescence**, for the treatment of **gastric ulcers** and **inflammation** of the stomach lining. More recent research shows that fenugreek seeds can also help lower **blood-sugar levels** in diabetics and that they may also slow down the spread of **liver tumours.**

how to use it

Seeds are usually added to food during cooking and can be used whole, lightly roasted and crushed or finely ground. They can also be sprouted, making a tangy and extremely healthy addition to salads.

ginger
zingiber officinale

what it is

Ginger is one of the greatest of all natural medicines, used by Chinese doctors since 1,000 BC and popular with European herbalists from the Middle Ages. The root of this extraordinary plant is used in both food and medicine, and it is reputed to have been one of God's gifts to man in the Garden of Eden. Ginger grows throughout China and the rest of Asia, in the tropics and South America. Although some inedible varieties make powerful anti-inflammatories, ginger is the only one in common usage.

dosage

Fresh grated root: 2 grams three to four times daily. Dried ginger powder: 1 gram three times daily. Capsules of standardized ginger extract: up to 1 gram daily.

precautions

There are no reports of adverse reactions with other medications. However, some people may initially suffer heartburn after taking ginger. Those with stomach ulcers, hiatus hernia or gastric reflux problems should start with small doses and always take ginger with food.

what it does

Ginger is one of the most potent of digestive remedies and an almost certain **cure** for various types of **nausea.** It is particularly effective for the relief of early morning sickness in pregnancy, and is safe for both mother and baby. It works equally well for the **prevention** and treatment of travel sickness, and is even used to prevent nausea after anaesthetics. **Migraine** sufferers can also benefit – providing they take their ginger before the onset of vomiting. The plant is gaining growing acceptance as an adjunct to radiotherapy and chemotherapy, both of which commonly cause severe nausea.

Ginger contains extremely **powerful,** active volatile oils which provide both its distinctive taste and smell as well as medicinal benefits. Zingiberene, zingerone, boreal, bisabolene and shogaols are the most important chemical constituents. These anti-inflammatory compounds are responsible for the other main medicinal value of ginger, which is as an **anti-inflammatory** for the treatment of rheumatism and arthritis. Although ordinary ginger does help with these conditions and is also an effective **circulatory booster**, other inedible Chinese varieties are even more potent.

how to use it

Fresh root: slice or grate into food, or grate 2.5 cm (½ in) into a mug, cover for 10 minutes and strain for tea. Powder can be more pungent than fresh root, and the volatile oils decline rapidly. Commercial ginger capsules are widely available.

liquorice

glycyrrhiza glabra

what it is

Another vitally important Chinese herbal medicine, the use of which dates back to antiquity. Liquorice grows wild in most of southern Europe and southwestern Asia, and the roots of three- to four-year-old plants are used medicinally and in the manufacture of sweets.

The plant is commercially cultivated in many places and was introduced to England by monks during the 16th century, most famously growing at Pontefract Castle where the liquorice sweets known as Pontefract cakes were created. Although no longer a commercial crop in England, liquorice grows well in the garden or in a large pot.

dosage

Deglycyrrhizinated liquorice (DGL): 200mg three times daily. Tincture of liquorice: 5ml in water three times daily. Liquorice root capsules: up to 5 grams daily.

precautions

Glycyrrhizin can cause fluid retention and raise blood pressure, so avoid long-term use of large doses: more than 10 grams of root. There are no reports of interactions with other medications. Not recommended during pregnancy, breast-feeding or for children under five. Use liquorice sweets sparingly in children over five to relieve tummy upsets; can cause diarrhoea.

what it does

The historic use of liquorice was as a treatment for digestive problems such as **gastritis**, mouth ulcers, **stomach ulcers** and over-acidity. Its natural demulcents (soothers) and **anti-inflammatories** line the digestive tract with a protective gel, which prevents inflammation and reduces the spasm of the gut's smooth muscle. It is also gently laxative. Modern research has shown that liquorice can also be useful in the treatment of **liver problems**, and stimulate the adrenal glands. The most important constituents are glycyrrhizin, **flavonoids**, coumarins and sterols. It is the glycyrrhic acid – 50 times sweeter than sugar – that accounts for the plant's popularity as a sweet.

how to use it

If you grow your own, dry the roots of three- to four-year-old plants and use them to make a tincture; add 5 to 250ml of water and drink a glass after each meal. Take as liquorice capsules. For mouth ulcers, open the capsule, add to a tumbler of warm water and use as a mouthwash; do not swallow.

available as

Dried leaves

Fresh leaves

Oil

Tablets

Tea bags

peppermint

mentha piperita

what it is

The use of peppermint certainly dates back to the ancient Egyptians, as leaves of the plant were found in the pyramids. The Greeks and the Romans both used it for flavour and its medicinal purposes, and the first record of it being cultivated in England was in the middle of the 18th century. It is a hybrid mint whose origins are unknown, but various varieties were used all over the world. The Japanese have extracted menthol from mint since the birth of Christ. This is one herb everyone should grow for its extraordinary digestive benefits. If you put it in the garden, knock the bottom out of an old bucket and plant inside the rim to stop it spreading. All mints grow easily in pots, and the more you cut them, the better they grow.

dosage

Pure oil of peppermint: two drops
to half a glass of warm water,
sip slowly. For tea, one teaspoon
of dried leaves or six fresh leaves
to a cup of boiling water. Tablets of
peppermint leaf: 4 to 6 grams daily.

precautions

There are no reports of interactions
with other medications, and the use
of peppermint in cooking or as tea
is safe even on a daily basis.
Large quantities of peppermint oil
may cause heartburn. Tea should
be made very weak for children
and not given to infants.

what it does

Peppermint is probably one of the most effective remedies for
indigestion and peppermint oil is still widely prescribed by
doctors and consultants for the relief of gastric discomfort. For
indigestion after meals, irritable bowel syndrome (IBS), flatulence,
colic or abdominal **cramp**, peppermint is a must. If your **appetite**
is flagging, it will come to the rescue. It is also good for the treatment
of tension **headaches** and helps boost **concentration** during
times of mental effort.

Volatile oils, mostly menthol and menthone, and the flavonoid
menthocide, are the key ingredients, which also help stimulate the
production of bile essential for the effective digestion of fatty foods.
Throughout the Middle East, a glass of mint tea is the traditional
drink after meals.

how to use it

Place a sprig of fresh mint
into a glass, add boiling
water, a slice of lemon
and a teaspoon of honey,
if desired. Preparations of
oil of peppermint are
available; use as a drink
in warm water. Apply to
the skin for the relief of
aches and pains: five
drops of peppermint oil to
100 ml of carrier oil (grape
or sunflower). Also take
as tablets made from
dried peppermint leaf.

healing
boosters

Ailment	Booster	Effect
Acne	Artichoke, Dandelion	Artichoke improves liver function and fat digestion. Dandelion is both cleansing and diuretic.
Anxiety	Passion-flower, Valerian	Both are calming and mild tranquilisers.
Arthritis	Devil's claw, Glucosamine, Pycnogenols	Devil's claw and pycnogenols are both anti-inflammatories, while glucosamine sulphate helps repair damaged cartilage.
Back pain	Chilli, Devil's claw	Chilli stimulates the circulation and promotes healing of damaged tissues. Devil's claw is a natural anti-inflammatory.
Boils	Garlic, Tea tree	Both are powerful anti-bacterials (eat one clove of garlic a day or take as tablets; apply tea tree oil directly to the boil).
Bruising	Horse chestnut, Pycnogenols	Horse chestnut improves capillary blood flow. Pycnogenols are natural anti-inflammatories.
Chilblains	Chilli, Ginger, Vitamin E	All stimulate and improve circulation to the extremities.
Cholesterol	Evening primrose oil, Folic acid, Garlic	Evening primrose oil is anti-inflammatory and protects the arteries. Folic acid controls levels of heart-damaging homocysteine. Garlic helps reduce blood cholesterol.
Chronic fatigue	BIO-STRATH Elixir, Coenzyme Q_{10}, Ginseng, St John's wort	BIO-STRATH is an immune booster, protects against infection and improves nutrient uptake. Coenzyme Q_{10} improves energy release from food. Ginseng boosts energy. St John's wort helps with depression that accompanies chronic fatigue.
Circulation problems	Ginger, Ginkgo biloba, Vitamin E	Ginger stimulates circulation and improves blood flow. Ginkgo biloba helps dilate the tiny capillaries at the end of the circulatory system. Vitamin E strengthens blood vessel walls.
Colds	Devil's claw, Echinacea, Lapacho	Devil's claw lessens aches and pains. Echinacea and lapacho are both immune boosters.

Ailment	Booster	Effect
Cough	Garlic, Liquorice, Valerian	Garlic is anti-bacterial. Liquorice is an effective expectorant. Valerian improves sleep that is interrupted by coughing.
Cramp	Chilli, Ginger, Vitamin E	All stimulate and improve circulation.
Cystitis	Cranberry, Dandelion	Cranberry protects against urinary bacteria. Dandelion is diuretic.
Depression	Kava kava, Lemon balm, St John's wort	Kava kava eases stress and anxiety. Lemon balm relieves physical tension. St John's wort helps moderate depression.
Fever	Chamomile, Feverfew, Tea tree	Chamomile helps ease fevers, especially for children. Tea tree is anti-bacterial. Feverfew helps lower body temperature.
Flatulence	Fennel, Peppermint	Both relieve symptoms.
Fluid retention	Dandelion	Dandelion leaves are a powerful diuretic.
Gallstones	Artichoke, Fenugreek	Artichoke stimulates the gall bladder and improves liver function. Fenugreek protects and stimulates the liver.
Gastritis	Chamomile, Fennel, Peppermint	Chamomile relieves stomach pain. Fennel seeds relieve gastric discomfort. Peppermint reduces stomach acidity.
Gout	Dandelion, Devil's claw, Lemon balm, Pycnogenols	Dandelion's diuretic action helps remove uric acid which causes the pain of gout. Devil's claw and pycnogenols are anti-inflammatories. Lemon balm relieves muscle spasms.
Hair problems	Chamomile, BIO-STRATH elixir, Red clover	BIO-STRATH improves nutrient absorption to aid hair health. Chamomile helps strengthen weak hair (drink as tea or use tea as a rinse after washing). Red clover provides plant hormones which may help reduce hair loss.
Headache	Artichoke, Dong quai, Feverfew	Artichoke cleanses the liver (good for hangover headaches). Dong quai relieves vascular spasm, so may help headaches associated with blood flow. Feverfew eases headaches.

Ailment	Booster	Effect
Heart disease	Folic acid, Garlic, Lycopene, Selenium, Vitamin E	Folic acid controls homocysteine levels, a predictor of heart disease. Garlic lowers blood pressure and cholesterol, and reduces the stickiness of blood. Lycopene is a protective antioxidant. Selenium is an essential mineral. Vitamin E protects both heart and arteries against oxidative damage.
Hepatitis	Artichoke, Milk thistle	Artichoke stimulates the liver and gall bladder and improves fat digestion. Milk thistle is useful for all liver problems.
Herpes	Garlic, Lemon balm	Both are specifically anti-viral. Dab the cut end of a garlic clove onto affected areas, eat garlic in food or take as tablets. Take lemon balm as tea; use cold tea as a lotion on any areas affected with the herpes virus.
Hypertension	Coenzyme Q$_{10}$, Flax seeds, Garlic	Coenzyme Q$_{10}$ may lead to significant reduction in blood pressure. Flax seed oil aids cholesterol and blood pressure reduction. Garlic lowers blood pressure and cholesterol.
Impotence	Catuaba, Muira Puama, Pfaffia	Catuaba stimulates the central nervous system. Muira Puama helps improve sexual function. Pfaffia helps combat stress.
Indigestion	Chamomile, Fennel seeds, Peppermint	Chamomile relieves stomach pain. Fennel seeds relieve flatulence. Peppermint reduces stomach acidity.
Influenza	Cat's claw, Echinacea, Turmeric	Cat's claw is a great immune booster. Echinacea protects against viruses. Turmeric is anti-bacterial and anti-viral.
Insomnia	Passion-flower, St John's wort, Valerian	Passion-flower is calmative. St John's wort is an anti-depressant; insomnia can be a symptom of depression. Valerian encourages deeper sleep and prevents waking in the small hours.
Memory loss	Ginkgo biloba, Phosphatidylserine	Ginkgo biloba stimulates blood flow to the smallest blood vessels of the brain, specifically improving short-term memory loss. Phosphatidylserine is a vital regulator of brain function and helps improve general memory.

Ailment	Booster	Effect
Menstrual problems	Black cohosh, Chamomile, Dandelion	Black cohosh helps regulate general physical and emotional disruptions of the menstrual cycle. Chamomile eases painful breasts before and during periods. Dandelion helps correct fluid retention, which causes menstrual discomfort.
Mouth ulcers	Garlic, Lemon balm, Probiotics	Garlic oil is excellent for healing mouth ulcers (rub the ulcers with the cut, squeezed end of a clove). Lemon balm is anti-viral and prevents secondary infections (use lemon balm tea as an anti-viral mouthwash). Probiotics replace the friendly bacteria in the mouth and digestive tract which protect against infections.
Prostate problems	Zinc & oyster extract	Zinc is essential for proper functioning of the prostate.
Raynaud's Syndrome	Chilli, Ginger, Ginkgo biloba, Vitamin E	All stimulate and improve circulation to the extremities.
Seasonal Affective Disorder (SAD)	Ginseng, Lemon balm, St John's wort	While none of these is a true treatment for the condition (light therapy is most effective), together they can produce a remarkable improvement. Ginseng provides an energy boost which at least enables sufferers to be more active. Lemon balm relaxes physical tension and aids well-being. St John's wort helps to overcome the inevitable depression of SAD.
Tired All The Time Syndrome	BIO-STRATH elixir, Guarana, Kelp, Schisandra	BIO-STRATH promotes well-being. Guarana provides a gentle, slow-release energy boost. Kelp stimulates the thyroid, which is commonly, though sub-clinically, underactive. Schisandra restores the zest for life and improves mental state.
Varicose veins	Chilli, Garlic, Ginger, Horse chestnut, Vitamin E	All stimulate and improve circulation to the extremities. Vitamin E in particular helps to strengthen vein walls.

booster
diets

aphrodisiac diet

Music may soothe the savage breast, but here's a menu guaranteed to result in consuming passion. This meal combines the best of heart-friendly foods with many of the traditional aphrodisiacs. The sexually enhancing qualities of these ingredients, combined with the appropriate aphrodisiac boosters, will transport you and your partner to a world of magical delight.

Oysters are the most famous of all aphrodisiac foods and can enhance any man's performance. Providing you and your lover like them, sharing a dozen with half a bottle of chilled Champagne will set the mood while putting the finishing touches to your feast of love.

Start with a celery, avocado, grape and pink grapefruit salad, topped with a dressing of raspberry vinegar, pink peppercorns, extra-virgin olive oil and a sprinkling of sesame seeds, decorated with sprigs of fresh coriander.

Follow this with grilled salmon steaks with a green sauce of gooseberries and fennel (sweat gooseberries in butter until tender and remove from pan, add a drop of Pernod to deglaze pan and mix in low-fat fromage frais to make a sauce, add the gooseberries and finely chopped fresh fennel), baby new potatoes boiled (skins on), steamed broccoli with thin strips of carrot, and a tiny watercress salad with walnut oil and lemon dressing.

Finish with a bowl of strawberries, and share half a bottle of pink Champagne. Go easy on the booze; a little works wonders, but don't forget the infamous 'brewer's droop'. As Shakespeare (paraphrased) warns men more subtly in *Macbeth*, 'Drink provokes the desire, but it takes away the performance.'

Throughout, add soft music and candles – but no coffee, which Voltaire described as the 'drink of eunuchs'.

immune booster

This four-day eating plan is perfect at times of stress, when resistance is lowered and when flu, coughs and colds are rampant. During the diet, drink at least 1 litre (1¾ pints) of water and at least another litre of fluids (herbal teas, unsweetened/unsalted fruit/vegetable juice, weak Indian or China tea) and coffee only occasionally.

Day 1
Breakfast Half a grapefruit, one poached egg and two poached tomatoes.
Lunch Avocado, tomato and mushroom salad plus 115g (4oz) of low-fat cottage cheese. A large bunch of grapes.
Dinner A large bowl of thinly sliced cucumber with lots of black pepper, cider vinegar and a teaspoon of extra-virgin olive oil. A generous portion of mixed stir-fried vegetables served on a bed of plain boiled rice.

Day 2
Breakfast A large fresh peach and six ripe strawberries.
Lunch A large green salad and a mixture of lots of steamed vegetables – carrots, courgettes, new potatoes, peas, runner beans, sweetcorn – tossed in a light teaspoon of butter and sprinkled with fresh chopped mint and parsley.
Dinner A bowl of vegetable soup. A large red or yellow pepper stuffed with rice, and a generous portion of lightly cooked, chopped spinach with a drizzle of extra-virgin olive oil and a clove of crushed garlic.

Day 3
Breakfast A large bowl of cherries and a small carton of live, low-fat natural yoghurt.
Lunch A mixed green salad. A generous portion of pasta topped with olive oil, crushed garlic and fresh parsley.
Dinner A small carton of live, low-fat natural yoghurt with chopped cucumber, fresh mint, garlic, black pepper and olive oil. One skinless grilled chicken breast, with grilled tomato, iceberg lettuce and boiled or baked potatoes.

Day 4
Breakfast Muesli or another wholegrain cereal with semi-skimmed milk, and a banana.
Lunch A sliced hard-boiled egg with chunks of tomato, cucumber, fennel and lettuce in wholemeal pitta bread.
Dinner A celery, apple and walnut salad. One grilled trout with cauliflower and runner beans tossed in a teaspoon of olive oil and a squeeze of lemon juice, sprinkled with lots of parsley.

big day diet

For maximum concentration and brain power during a stressful time, it's best to reverse some normal eating patterns. The object of this exercise is to be at peak performance during the morning and afternoon, and to unwind, relax and sleep well during the evening and night. If exams are just around the corner, it's no good trying to sit up until the small hours and cram; if you don't know it by now, you never will!

The same eating plan will sharpen your concentration and keep your brain in top gear for important interviews, crucial business meetings or vital social events. Combined with the mood boosters that suit your needs, you'll have no worries – whatever the occasion.

Nutritionally perfect for extended periods of brain work, the daily diet below provides approximately 2,000 calories, lots of protein, low carbohydrates, low fat, low salt and well over the recommended daily requirement of each essential nutrient. Follow this and your mind will be fully alert when you need it most.

Breakfast This should include high-protein, low-fat and little carbohydrate, so...
A large glass of fresh orange or pineapple juice. One small carton of live, low-fat natural yoghurt with toasted almonds or pistachios. A poached egg with baked beans and an apple or pear.
Mid-morning A snack of dried apricots, raisins, dates and plain fresh nuts.
Lunch A mixed salad with cold meat, fish or low-fat cheese. Add sesame seeds, sunflower seeds and pumpkin seeds to the salad, and include plenty of watercress and tomatoes.
Mid-afternoon A piece of low-fat cheese (if you haven't had it already today) or a hard-boiled egg with an apple, pear or bunch of grapes.
Evening meal A thick, root-vegetable casserole made with potatoes, swede, parsnip, turnip, carrot, onion, celery, shredded cabbage, canned kidney beans and rice or barley, or a generous portion of pasta or risotto with your favourite low-fat sauce. Finish with a delicious carbohydrate-rich rice pudding – add plenty of nutmeg. During the evening, eat a banana and a few dates or dried apricots.

NOTE: If your mental faculties are needed in the evening, and you want a calm, peaceful day, stick to cereals and bread for breakfast, the starch meal for lunch and the high-protein meal for dinner.

powerhouse diet

These three days feature mouthwatering recipes that taste good, look good and do you good. Vitality eating is yours for the cooking, and once you've experienced the energy surge provided by these vital foods, you'll want to use them at least one or two days each week as part of your normal eating plan.

If lack of energy is a problem, don't miss out on the vitality boosters that help achieve peak performance. Never skip breakfast and don't go more than three hours without food: always have a banana and a bag of unsalted fresh nuts, raisins and dried apricots handy to satisfy hunger pangs, but be sure to avoid the doughnuts and chocolate.

In addition to the menus below, drink at least 1½ to 2½ litres (approximately 3 to 4 pints) of fluid – herbal tea or water – a day to flush out the system, protect against cystitis and keep your skin in good condition. Avoid caffeine, too – you're better off without it.

Day 1

Breakfast Sliced blood oranges and pink grapefruit. A small carton of live, low-fat natural yoghurt, sprinkled with a teaspoon of chopped nuts and a teaspoon of honey.

Lunch Scrambled eggs with mushrooms on a bed of mixed salad leaves. Dried-fruit compôte: add boiling water, a rosehip tea bag, a tablespoon of honey and two cloves to a bowl of mixed dried fruits – prunes, apricots, figs, apple rings, pears, peaches, etc. Cover and leave to stand overnight. Remove the tea bag and serve with a sprinkle of flaked almonds.

Dinner Stuffed peppers: one red and one yellow pepper stuffed with brown rice, raisins, onion, parsley, mint and pine nuts and cooked. Serve with crusty wholemeal bread. For dessert, some fresh dates and figs.

Day 2

Breakfast Dried-fruit compôte with a small carton of live, low-fat natural yoghurt and an orange.

Lunch Half an avocado, sliced, with watercress, tomatoes and cucumber, on mixed leaves, sprinkled with a generous squeeze of lemon juice. One crusty wholewheat roll.

Dinner: Mustard marinated salmon

salmon steaks	4, about 175g (6oz) each

For the marinade:

olive oil	2 tablespoons, extra-virgin
onion	2 tablespoons, finely chopped
dry white wine	4 tablespoons
salt and pepper	to taste
Dijon mustard	2 tablespoons

To garnish:
lemon slices
fresh coriander sprigs

1 Shake marinade ingredients in a screw-top jar, then pour into a large, shallow dish.
2 Add salmon steaks, coat with marinade and refrigerate for approximately three hours, turning them once.
3 Heat the grill. Grease the rack with a little oil, put fish in place and brush each steak with some of the marinade. Cook for about four minutes on each side at maximum heat.
4 Serve garnished with lemon and coriander, with puréed spinach, seasoned with nutmeg.

For dessert, have a selection of vitality-boosting tropical fruits: pineapple, mango, kiwi fruit, pawpaw and passion-fruit.

Day 3

A meatless day, just to show that being vegetarian isn't all brown rice and lentils. Vegetarians are less likely to have high blood pressure, heart disease, gallstones, constipation, piles and bowel cancer, so why not give it a try? You might like it, and your body certainly will.

This is also a heart-friendly day, with little cholesterol or saturated fat, a low dose of salt but plenty of heart-protective monounsaturated fats. Lots of vitality vitamins are guaranteed to put a spring in your step.

Breakfast Two hot wholewheat rolls spread with a little butter and a banana.

Lunch: Risotto con salsa cruda

long-grain brown rice	250g (9oz)
salt	a pinch
tomatoes	4 medium
cucumber	½ medium
garlic	2 cloves
spring onions	4 medium
carrots	4 medium
radishes	4 medium
courgettes	3 small
peas	1 tablespoon, fresh or frozen
olive oil	125ml (4floz) extra-virgin
sea salt	to taste
black pepper	freshly ground, to taste
chives	chopped, to taste
parsley	chopped, to taste

1 Wash rice and cook gently in twice its volume of boiling, slightly salted water, covered, for about 40 minutes. Check occasionally but don't stir.

2 When cooked, remove from heat, then leave uncovered for 10 minutes, until dry and separated.

3 Chop tomatoes. Peel and dice cucumber. Finely chop garlic, spring onions, carrots, radishes and courgettes. Place in a bowl with peas, add oil and season lightly. Marinate for 30 minutes.

4 While the rice is warm, place in bowl, add the vegetable mixture and stir gently. Season to taste, sprinkle with chopped herbs and serve with green salad.

For dessert, have a mixture of some raisins and nuts.

Dinner: Aubergine caviar with crudités

aubergines	2 large
lemon	juice of 1 large
olive oil	3 tablespoons extra-virgin
garlic	1 clove
natural yoghurt	2 tablespoons live, low-fat

sea salt	to taste
black pepper	freshly ground, to taste
coriander seeds	½ teaspoon, crushed

1 Heat oven to 200°C (400°F/gas mark 6). Bake aubergines until soft (about 20 minutes), cut open, and scrape flesh into a bowl. Add lemon juice to flesh and beat in oil, drop by drop, to form a smooth cream.

2 Crush garlic and stir into the bowl with yoghurt. Season with salt, pepper and crushed coriander seeds. Stir well, cover and chill for an hour.

3 Serve with crudités – strips of carrot, celery, cucumber, fennel, sprigs of cauliflower. There'll be lots left over for a healthy nibble.

Veggieballs in tomato sauce

veggie-burger mix	500g (1lb 2oz)
egg	1 medium
olive oil	2 tablespoons, extra virgin
garlic	3 cloves, chopped
fresh mint and parsley	2 tablespoons each, chopped
black pepper	freshly ground, to taste

For the tomato sauce:

tinned chopped tomatoes	1 x 400g (14oz)
vegetable stock cube	1
dry white wine	2 tablespoons
onion	1 large, chopped
olive oil	1 tablespoon, extra-virgin
green chilli	1, deseeded and chopped

1 For the sauce, put tomatoes and their juice in a wok with the crumbled stock cube, wine, onion, oil and chilli. Bring to simmering point, cover and let bubble for 10 minutes, stirring occasionally.

2 Make up the veggie-burger mix as directed on the packet. Add garlic, fresh herbs and pepper.

3 Form into table-tennis size balls and fry gently until browned all over and cooked through.

4 Add to the tomato sauce and serve on a bed of green pasta.

three-day detox diet

This three-day plan is pretty low in calories. You will feel hungry from time to time, but don't spoil the effect by cheating. You won't be drinking coffee – only very weak tea without milk or sugar – so your caffeine intake will come to an abrupt halt. The combination of less food, no coffee and the effects of detoxification will almost certainly cause a headache. Drink masses of water and try to avoid painkillers: the headache is transient, and by day four you'll feel absolutely great – full of protective antioxidants.

Plan the first two days of the diet for a time when your workload is at its lightest. To help overcome hunger pangs, take two teaspoons of the swiss herbal tonic BIO-STRATH elixir three times a day and, if you don't have a juicer, Biotta organic vegetable juices, which are salt-free and delicious.

Regular use of the cleansing boosters will help keep your system working efficiently. Adding dandelion leaves and Jerusalem artichokes to salads and vegetable dishes during this diet has specific effects on the kidneys and liver.

In addition to the menus below, be sure to drink at least 2-3 litres (4 pints) of fluids – water, weak black tea or herbal tea – each day.

Day 1: approximately 512 calories

This first detox day is designed to kick-start your metabolism into action, providing more than the daily requirement of folic acid, niacin, potassium, vitamins B_1, B_6, A, C and E, the powerful and protective antioxidants.

Breakfast One orange, half a grapefruit, a large slice of melon. A glass of unsalted vegetable juice. A cup of herbal tea with honey.

Lunch A plate of raw red and yellow peppers, cucumber, tomato, broccoli, cauliflower, celery, carrots, radishes and lots of fresh parsley with extra-virgin olive oil and lemon juice dressing. One large glass of unsweetened fruit juice.

Dinner A large mixed salad – lettuce, tomato, watercress, onion, garlic, beetroot, celeriac, fresh mint and any other herbs you like – drizzled with extra-virgin olive oil and lemon juice. One large glass of unsweetened fruit juice or unsalted vegetable juice.

Day 2: approximately 1,226 calories

This second day of the diet provides more than the daily requirement of copper, folic acid, magnesium, phosphorus, potassium, vitamin B, B, A, C and E, and a good supply of protein, calcium, fibre, iron and selenium.

Breakfast One large glass of hot water with a thick slice of lemon and a tablespoon of honey. One small carton of live, low-fat, natural yoghurt.

Mid-morning One large glass of vegetable juice. A handful each of raisins, dried apricots and fresh nuts.

Lunch A salad of grated carrot, red cabbage and apple with sliced red pepper, tomato, radishes and celery, sprinkled with sunflower seeds, lemon juice and olive oil. A cup of herbal or weak Indian tea with honey (no milk).

Mid-afternoon One glass of fruit juice. One banana.

Dinner Any three cooked vegetables (excluding potatoes) drizzled with olive oil, nutmeg and lemon juice. A cup of herbal or weak Indian tea.

Evening snack A mixture of dried fruits and unsalted nuts and as much fresh fruit as you like.

Day 3: approximately 1,088 calories

This final day provides more than the daily requirements of copper, fibre, folic acid, magnesium, niacin, phosphorus, potassium, vitamins A, B₁, B₂, B₃, C and E, also lots of vitamin B₁₂, calcium and iron.

Breakfast A fresh fruit salad of apple, pear, grapes, mango and pineapple. One carton of live, low-fat natural yoghurt with a tablespoon of unsweetened muesli. A cup of herbal or weak Indian tea.

Mid-morning Six dried apricots. One glass of fruit or vegetable juice.

Lunch Lettuce soup: soften half a chopped onion in a large pan with a little olive oil; add half a shredded iceberg lettuce, stir; add 850ml (1½ pints) vegetable stock and lots of black pepper; simmer for 20 minutes; sprinkle with a handful of chopped parsley. A chunk of crusty wholemeal bread. A cup of herbal tea.

Mid-afternoon An apple and a pear.

Dinner Pasta with lettuce pesto: process the rest of the iceberg with a handful of pine nuts, a little olive oil, one clove of garlic and a carton of low-fat fromage frais. Tomato, onion and yellow pepper salad. A cup of herbal or weak Indian tea.

Treat your system gently on day four. Avoid red meat and start with plainly cooked chicken or fish, some starchy foods and plenty of fruit, salads and vegetables. Don't eat dairy products (apart from live yoghurt) until day five. If necessary, you can repeat the detox after two weeks, but do not follow it more than eight times a year and not more than twice in any three-month period.

glossary

Alkaloid Any nitrogen-containing organic bases obtained from plants.

Age-related macular degeneration (AMD) Gradual degeneration of the macula, the tissue making up the central portion of the retina, that can lead to blindness.

Anaemia A lessening of red blood cells, usually due to iron deficiency.

Antioxidant A substance that inhibits oxidation. In the body, antioxidants are thought to prevent the destruction of vitamin C, slow the destruction of body cells and strengthen the immune system.

B complex Water soluble vitamins other than vitamin C.

Beta-carotene A powerful antioxidant transformed by the body into vitamin A.

Bile Bitter, greenish-yellow fluid produced by the liver and stored in the gall bladder; also known as gall. Bile helps in the digestion and absorption of fats; it also neutralizes stomach acid.

Cholesterol Steroid substance manufactured by the body, which dissolves in fat and can contribute to hardening of the arteries, resulting in strokes or heart attacks. There are both 'good' and 'bad' types of cholesterol.

Colic A sharp, intermittent pain in the abdomen, most common in babies around three months old; can also occur in adults.

Colitis Inflammation of the colon, or large intestine.

Coumarin A white substance that beneficially affects blood flow.

Diuretic Any substance that causes increased urine discharge.

Diverticulitis Inflammation of the pouches of the intestinal walls by waste matter, which can lead to blockage of the colon.

DNA (deoxyribonucleic acid) A complicated nucleic acid structure that forms the basis of the chromosomes of living cells – the 'building blocks' of all life.

Endorphin Any of a group of hormones secreted by the brain, with tranquillizing or painkilling effects.

Enzyme A substance secreted by living cells, which breaks complex substances down for use in the body.

Epstein-Barr A herpes virus that causes mononucleosis (glandular fever) and may possibly be a factor in rheumatoid arthritis.

Flavonoid A beneficial phytochemical that tends to occur in plants high in vitamin C.

Free radical Naturally occurring oxygen molecules that damage the body and are thought to play a significant role in the ageing process.

Gastric reflux Condition arising when the acidic stomach contents flow back into the upper part of the oesophagus and gullet, causing a burning sensation and heartburn.

Gastroenteritis Inflammation of the stomach and intestines, which may be caused by a virus, bacterial infection, chemicals or lactose intolerance.

Glycoside Any of a group of organic compounds that produce sugars and related substances.

Hiatus hernia Painful condition – part of the stomach protrudes through the diaphragm, causing backflow.

Interferon A protein produced in cells that prevents duplication of infectious viruses.

International unit A means of expressing a recommended dosage of vitamins in terms of their activity; mainly used for vitamins A and E.

Irritable bowel syndrome (spastic colon or mucous colitis). A disorder producing various symptoms that chiefly affect the large intestine, or colon. Symptoms include pain, cramping, alternating diarrhoea and constipation, bloating and nausea.

Myalgic encephalomyelitis A condition that usually follows a viral infection, involving tiredness, muscle pain, lack of concentration, panic attacks, memory loss and depression.

Microgram Unit of weight equivalent to $\frac{1}{1000}$ of a milligram.

Phospholipids One of a group of essential nutrients essential for the proper structure of the cell membranes.

Polyphenol Organic compound, such as tannin, that combines with iron and can hinder its absorption.

Polyunsaturated fat Fat containing a high percentage of fatty acids deficient in hydrogen atoms, but containing extra carbon bonds. Of more benefit to the body than saturated fat.

Proanthocyanidin One of the powerful plant antioxidants particularly protective against cancer and heart disease.

Spina bifida Birth defect that affects the nerve tube in the spinal cord.

Tincture An alcohol solution of medicine.

Tired All The Time Syndrome A condition of constant lethargy, frequently associated with zinc and other nutritional deficiencies; though may be triggered by depression, or other underlying illness.

Varicose veins Condition in which vein valves malfunction, usually causing veins to swell and twist.

Volatile oil An essential oil derived from a plant and bearing its characteristic odour.

sources and further reading

Balick, Michael J and Cox, Paul Alan *Plants, People and Culture.* New York: American Library, 1996.

Chevallier, Andrew *The Encyclopaedia of Medicinal Plants.* London: Dorling Kindersley, 1996.

Daniel, C W and Wren FLS, R C *Potter's New Cyclopaedia of Botanical Drugs and Preparations.* Saffron Walden: The C W Daniel Company, 1998.

Grieve, Mrs M *A Modern Herbal.* Adelaide: Australia Savvas, 1984.

Griffith, Dr H W *The Vital Vitamin Fact File.* Wellingborough: Thorsons Publishing, 1988.

Griggs, Barbara *New Green Pharmacy.* London: Vermilion, 1997.

Griggs, Barbara *The Green Witch.* London: Vermilion, 1993.

Lininger, Skye *The Natural Pharmacy.* London: Prima Health, 1998.

McVicar, Jekka *Jekka's Complete Herb Book.* London: Kyle Cathie, 1994.

Murray, Michael and Pizzorno, Joseph *The Encyclopaedia of Natural Medicine.* London: Optima, 1995.

Norman, Jill *The Classic Herb Cookbook.* London: Dorling Kindersley, 1997.

Ody, Penelope *The Handbook of Over The Counter Herbal Medicines.* London: Kyle Cathie, 1996.

Page, Mary and Stearn, William T *Culinary Herbs: A Wisley Handbook.* London: The Royal Horticultural Society/Cassell and Co, 1988.

Physicians Desk Reference for Herbal Medicines. New Jersey: Medical Economics Company, 1999.

Sharon, Michael (Dr) *Complete Nutrition.* London: Prion, 1997.

Stuart, Malcolm (Dr) *Encyclopaedia of Herbs and Herbalism.* Edgerton International, 1994.

Taylor, Leslie *Herbal Secrets of the Rain Forest.* London: Prima Health, 1998.

van Straten, Michael *Foods for Mind and Body.* London: Harper Collins, 1997.

van Straten, Michael *Guarana – The Energy Seeds and Herbs of the Amazon Rain Forest.* Saffron Walden: The C W Daniel Company, 1994.

van Straten, Michael *The Family Medicine Chest.* London: Weidenfeld and Nicolson, 1998.

Williams, Tom *The Complete Illustrated Guide to Chinese Medicine.* Shaftsbury: Element, 1996.

index

Page numbers in **bold** type refer to main entries.